FIREPROOF

YOUR LIFE

FOR

TEENS

MICHAEL CATT

with AMY PARKER

B&H
PUBLISHING GROUP

NASHVILLE, TENNESSEE

FIREPROOF

YOUR LIFE

FOR

TEENS

MICHAEL CATT

with AMY PARKER

NASHVILLE, TENNESSEE

978-1-4336-8487-6

Published by B&H Publishing Group
Nashville, Tennessee

Dewey Decimal Classification: 248.83
Subject Heading: CHRISTIAN LIFE \ TEENAGERS \
FAITH

1 2 3 4 5 6 7 8 9 • 18 17 16 15

Dedicated to the middle and high school students who were part of the youth ministries when I served at First Baptist Church (Yukon, Oklahoma), First Baptist North Spartanburg (Spartanburg, South Carolina), Roswell Street Baptist Church (Marietta, Georgia), and Sagamore Hill Baptist Church (Fort Worth, Texas).

Thank you for letting me pour into your lives during those formidable years. Praying your faith is still standing up to the fires of life.

Contents

*"Fireproof doesn't mean that the fires
will never come, but that when they do,
you'll be able to withstand them."*
—FROM THE FILM *FIREPROOF*

Fireproof Your Life

Several years ago, I had the privilege of working together with my church to produce a film called *Fireproof*. The popularity and success of that film surprised us all. However, it also made one thing certain: we as Christians are continually seeking ways to galvanize our faith against the fires of the world around us.

There is arguably no time in your life when your faith is more under fire than your teenage years. But I'm here to tell you: as you struggle to find your place in this world, to learn who you are, you can only forge an indestructible identity by remembering *Whose* you are.

Using Bible-based teachings and practical applications, these next ten chapters will walk you through the process of building an invincible, impenetrable faith. This is not a faith that just shows up on Sunday mornings, but one that reaches deep into your heart and stretches out to encompass every area of your life. From decision-making to relationships to money, I pray that I can show you how a fireproof faith and biblical principles play an integral part in every aspect of your day-to-day life, as well as in shaping your future.

We tend to make life so complicated. Trials and temptations will come, but the solution is simple. For every single situation we are going to face, for every decision we are going to make, the answer is there. And it begins and ends with God.

So, whether you're facing the fires right now or just want to prepare for the inevitable, this book will hand you the tools and protection you need to face the fires of life. But only you can use them.

Don't give up. Don't give in. And don't back down. Like Shadrach, Meshach, and Abednego in that famous fiery furnace, when we learn to stand with God, we can all be fireproof.

I pray that this book shows you how. And I pray that your life and the lives of those around you grow forever stronger in your faith as you learn to fireproof your life.

Blessings,
Michael Catt

CHAPTER I

Standing in the Fire

O God, You are my God; I shall seek You earnestly;
My soul thirsts for You, my flesh yearns for You,
In a dry and weary land where there is no water.

—PSALM 63:1 NASB

When a forest fire rages across the mountainside of California, the giant sequoias that have been there for centuries are rarely destroyed. They take their stand. While other less hearty trees are consumed by the sweeping fire, the sequoia has, over hundreds of years, developed multiple layers of bark in preparation for the fire drill.[1]

These giant trees, some of which date back to the time of Christ, survive because of several self-protective elements.

For one, some of these trees have bark that is *two feet thick*. Still, after a fire, a tree can smolder for six to twelve months from the trauma of the flames that lashed at the bark.

When fires rage through our lives, we often find ourselves smoldering. We end up asking God, "Why this?" or "Why me?" We can even buy into the lie: "If God loved me, He wouldn't have allowed this to happen." But it is wrong to assume that God does not love us, doesn't care, or doesn't know what we're going through. The reality is that—regardless of our standing with God—we all go through fires and times of testing. These trials show what we are made of. They reveal our hearts, our faith, and our level of maturity.

And would you believe that the fires in the sequoia forests even promote *new* life? When the cone of the sequoia is burned, it dries out, pops open, and disperses its seeds. Each of those little cones—about the size of your pinky finger—contains up to two hundred seeds! The wind carries those seeds and deposits them on the ground as silently as snowflakes. And just as beautifully, new life springs from death; the torment of the flames results in the promise of new life.

A Cultivated Heart

Ironically, however, many of these forests contain no young trees. If fire opens a cone which produces two hundred seeds, and one tree can produce tens of thousands of cones, why isn't there any new growth? Where are all the young sequoia trees?

Unfortunately, over the years, tourists and onlookers have hardened the ground with trampling feet. So if no one cultivates or breaks up the soil, the seeds cannot take root and multiply. The key to the survival of the seeds is the nitrogen-rich soil, produced by layer upon layer of ash left by fires. But if the soil is so hard that even a tiny seed cannot sink in, the life within that seed simply wastes away on top of the hardened ground.

Do you remember Jesus' parable that talks about hardened soil? His parable of the sower holds great truths about fireproofing your life. He tells us how we can live a life that withstands the fire and produces new fruit, new life.

Take a look:

> "Consider the sower who went out to sow. As he was sowing, some seeds fell along the path, and the birds came and ate them up. Others fell on rocky ground, where there wasn't much soil, and they sprang up quickly since the soil wasn't deep. But when the sun came up they were scorched, and since they had no root, they withered. Others fell among thorns, and the thorns came up and choked them. Still others fell on good ground and produced a crop: some 100, some 60, and some 30 times what was sown." (Matthew 13:3–8)

In this parable the sower represents Jesus, the seed is the Word, and the soil is our hearts. We would all agree that the sower and the seed are both good, right? But the soil—our hearts—determines the fruit that is produced.

Take a moment to consider Jesus' explanation of the parable:

> "When anyone hears the word about the kingdom and doesn't understand it, the evil one comes and snatches away what was sown in his heart. This is the one sown along the path. And the one sown on rocky ground—this is one who hears the word and immediately receives it with joy. Yet he has no root in himself, but is short-lived. When pressure or persecution comes because of the word, immediately he stumbles. Now the one sown among the thorns—this is the one who hears the word, but the worries of this age and the seduction of wealth choke the word, and it becomes unfruitful. But the one sown on the good ground—this is one who hears and understands the word, who does bear fruit and yields: some 100, some 60, some 30 times what was sown." (Matthew 13:19–23)

Do any of these sound familiar? Have you seen (or been) the one who starts out following Jesus but eventually falls by the wayside? The one who stops going to church? Resorts to bad habits again? Or simply disengages in general? The

Devil finds a way to trip up these people, and they end up feeling so guilty and ashamed that they may never return to the forgiveness of Jesus. One minute they're praising God; the next minute they're blaming Him. The seed of the Word never took root, so when the fires come through pain or persecution, these guys blow it.

Others never mature because they get drawn in by the things of the world. Fame, fortune, popularity, and pleasure dominate their thinking. They get caught up in who's got what. They think only of themselves and protecting the stuff they have and accumulating more stuff they don't need. Whatever faith they had cultivated, they trade it all for what the world has to offer.

And these aren't just a few isolated cases. Did you notice that most of the time the seeds in the parable don't bear fruit? The only seeds that bear fruit are those sown in good soil, tended soil, soil that is conducive to bearing fruit. Jesus Himself knows how rare and how difficult it is to find soil that is ready to produce good fruit. And maybe that's why He not only tells the parable to His disciples, but also follows it up with a careful explanation just to make sure we all understand. He wanted them—and us, His disciples today—to know how to flourish in our own lives and how to reach out to others too.

Is there a part of the parable that you identify with the most? Do you recognize your friends in any of those descriptions? Regardless of your answers, no matter what condition *your* soil is in, we are starting—right now—to cultivate better soil, to prepare for the sower, and to yield a better harvest.

When Trouble Strikes

The bark of the sequoia is equipped with a natural fire retardant, a substance called tannin that acts to neutralize the burning embers that embed themselves in the tree. Another advantage of the sequoia is its height. The fire can only attack the base, the foundation of the tree, while the crown of the tree remains above the flames and is only singed by heat and smoke.

But this advantage also invites opposition. Because these trees stand tall, they are prone to lightning strikes, leaving them with hundreds of scars as proof of their battle for survival. Some of these strikes cut deep and cause parts of the tree to become useless, but the tree as a whole continues to live. Even the most powerful strikes on the most vulnerable areas of the tree can rarely destroy it, although it can take years to overcome the assault.

Another enemy well known for its attacks on the sequoias lies in wait for the right moment to attack. Once fire has heated and softened the bark, the California horntailed wasp bores into the bark and feeds on the beneficial insects living there. The fire-wasp, as it's commonly called, will then try to bore into the heart of the tree and deposit deadly larvae deep within the inner layers.

Even the strongest and tallest among us have been bruised and battered and burned by life. Like the bore of the fire-wasp, the scars run deep. But through the power of God and His Holy Spirit, we can learn to endure and to keep standing tall—we can learn to fireproof our lives.

Standing Tall

When God was looking for righteous men, he turned to men like Noah, Daniel, and Job. Something in those men enabled them to withstand their trials and to stand the test of time. One stood for God during a flood. One stood for God in the lions' den and in a pagan nation. One stood for God throughout unthinkable loss and sickness.

Noah, Daniel, and Job took many hits. They were laughed at and criticized; Job was even told to curse God and die. They probably faced moments when they wondered if it was all worth it, but they survived their times of testing. Job was blameless and upright and feared God. Although he lost so much that was precious to him, he never cursed God. Although Job's friends gave endless reasoning for his condition, he waited for God to answer. Through it all, these men stood strong.

And today we are still looking to them as examples of strength.

Like these Old Testament giants, the sequoia has what it takes to stand the test of time. Over the years, the sequoias drop their lower branches through wind, fire, lightning, or by some other natural process. They let go of the things unfit for a mature tree. Even the upper branches are thinned out until only a few of the strongest and most strategically placed are held in a dome-like crown to absorb the maximum amount of sun and rain. They simplify down to only what is important for sustaining life and purpose.

When the sequoia is old—after being struck by lightning, attacked by fires, stung by wasps, and weathered by thousands of snowstorms—it stands resolute above all others, distinctive and majestic in its beauty. The branches are eight to ten feet in diameter. The roots run in a network reaching more than two hundred feet in width. The great sequoias are not deformed by harsh weather; the strongest, most direct winds actually *strengthen* the trees instead of weaken them. As believers, if rooted in Christ, the winds of adversity will do the same for us.

Even more impressive than its size is the longevity of this remarkable tree. Millennium after millennium, whatever the forces may deliver, sequoias triumph over tempest and fire and time, fruitful and beautiful, giving food and shelter to multitudes of small creatures dependent on their bounty.

What about you? Do you share the sequoia's secret? Do you have the resolve to live a fireproof life? The tests will come. Others will fail, and you may find yourself in a hard winter of discouragement. Some may whisper in your ear that serving God is not worth it.

Stand up. Stand strong. Stand tall.

It's time to fireproof your life.

Fire Drill!

1. Think of the many forces that act against the health of the sequoia tree. How can those relate to the forces you feel against you every day?

2. Like the sequoia, what protective elements or measures can you use to guard against the wind and weather that come your way?

3. Which part of Jesus' parable best describes where you are right now? Be honest. It's important to know where you are, in order to know where to go from here. Think about your friends. Can you think of one to fit each of the parable's descriptions?

4. How could Jesus' explanation help you—and your friends—to cultivate your lives to be more receptive to His Word?

5. What can you do today to start developing better soil?

CHAPTER 2

Fireproof Your Life—
Right Now!

For the LORD watches over the way of the righteous,
but the way of the wicked leads to ruin.

—PSALM 1:6

F or a number of years, I had the privilege of serving
   with two other men on the board of the contemporary
Christian group 4Him. Along with our wives, we were
asked to give advice, counsel, and accountability to one of
the most popular and successful groups of the century. One
year at a Gospel Music Association panel discussion prior
to the Dove Awards, one member of the group summed up

how valuable the board was in his eyes: "If it weren't for the accountability board, we probably wouldn't be together right now."

During those board meetings we learned to pray, to get honest with each other, to hold each other accountable, and to grow together. Whether you're a popular Christian band or just a teen trying to survive high school, this is what true Christian fellowship is. If I want to fireproof my life, I must be open to constructive criticism, suggestions, and insight from other believers. If I'm not teachable, I'll lose my footing at some point on my journey.

All of us know that relationships are tested, whether in a singing group, a friendship, or a family. How we respond to those tests can determine whether we are a success or a statistic. I want my life to be a story of God's faithfulness and my obedience. I don't want to be another casualty. I want to be someone my family can be proud of, a good friend, a strong leader, a Christ follower.

One of my favorite songs recorded by 4Him was entitled "A Man You Would Write About."

From the time time began
You always chose a man
To lead the people safely by Your way
To be a voice and echo what You say

Like David or Abraham
Your Word is full of such men
And if the Bible had no closing page
And still was being written to this day

I want to be a man that you would write about
A thousand years from now that they could read about
Your servant of choice in whom You found favor
A man who heard Your voice

Generations away it is my prayer
That they will look back and say,
"Oh, to have that kind of faith and love.
What a solid man of God he was."[1]

Success by God's Standards

When celebrities make the news or people around us are talked about, it's mostly news about their failures and down-falls. We'll read about the latest singer going into drug rehab or athletes getting caught using performance-enhancing drugs. You hear the sad tales of pastors lured into pornography or parents getting divorced. The casualties are so common that we are no longer shocked when people fall. In fact, we've come to expect it and accept it as normal.

On the other hand, you don't have to look far to find books, articles, and TV shows defining success, telling us how to get it (quick!), and highlighting people who embody the idea. The people highlighted are usually those impacting and changing America. They're being recognized for taking risks, having initiative, or being creative and persistent.

But really, that type of "success" is centered around selfishness and a rejection of the biblical worldview. Little is mentioned or praised when it comes to morals, integrity, biblical values, or character. In fact, more and more often, people are coming under fire for standing up for their biblical beliefs. A quick look at today's "success" stories makes it clear that success doesn't really involve the condition of the heart. And most books and shows trying to sell you on their formula for success make it seem like an unattainable secret that only *they* hold the keys to, so that you have to read their book or watch their show to learn their complicated, mystical secret.

God, however, sees things differently. He has made it really clear what qualities He is looking for in an individual. In the Bible's description of success, there are obvious characteristics to follow and observations to be noted.

The first psalm defines success in terms of character, not vocation. Success isn't about money; it's about lasting value. This psalm gives us a vivid contrast between the righteous and the wicked, a pattern seen consistently through Scripture: saved and lost, blessed and cursed, wise and foolish.

The reason lives go up in smoke is that people believe there is middle ground. We have bought the lie that compromise is acceptable. If a person does not make the Word of God his guide, the way of God his aim, and the will of God his one desire, he will *always* be susceptible to failure.

If, however, we want to live a blessed life that is pleasing to the Lord—a God-standard of success—there are specific things that must be part of our daily living. We must pay attention to what God says and apply it to the way we live our lives. If we want to survive the fires of life, we'll have to start fireproofing from the inside out. We have to fireproof our motives, why we make the choices we make, and ultimately, what ideas are driving those choices.

In *Fireproof*, Caleb begins to realize this in a conversation with his father.

EXT. WOODED PATH
CALEB walks beside JOHN.

> **CALEB**
> Dad, I'm glad you didn't split up . . .
> but I would've understood if you had.

> **JOHN**
> Do you know why we didn't?

> **CALEB**
> Not really. She realized she couldn't
> do any better?

> **JOHN**
> (smiles) Not quite. Caleb, the Lord did
> a work in us, in both of us.

> **CALEB**
> The Lord? (stops and looks at JOHN)
> You—you're giving credit to God?

> **JOHN**
> Why does that bother you?
> You've always believed in God.

CALEB
(takes deep breath) If there's a God out there somewhere, Dad, he's not interested in me and my problems.

JOHN
I disagree. I'd say he's very interested.

CALEB
Then where's he been in my life?

JOHN
I'd say he's been at work all around you. You just haven't realized it. (pauses) You haven't exactly given him an open invitation.

People are looking for happiness and blessing. Unfortunately, they often look in the wrong places, causing them to get off track and ultimately fall. They stumble along the way because they look anywhere but to the Lord for peace, joy, and happiness. We seal our fate by the choices we make.

Consider Matthew 7:13: "Enter through the narrow gate. For the gate is wide and the road is broad that leads to destruction, and there are many who go through it." Although those words were written about two thousand years ago, aren't they still true today? Following the Word of God and His values is not usually the popular path. But His Word that was true two thousand years ago is true today and will be true two thousand years from now. And when you think of it that way, which road would you rather be on?

Psalm 1 begins with a blessing and ends with a curse. It is a passionate declaration of the psalmist to seek the ways of God and a warning to avoid the ways of the wicked. It is an Old Testament prequel to Paul's words in 1 Corinthians: "So, whoever thinks he stands must be careful not to fall" (10:12).

Wicked, Sinners, and Scoffers—Oh My!

> How blessed is the man who does not walk in the counsel of the wicked, Nor stand in the path of sinners, Nor sit in the seat of scoffers! (Psalm 1:1 NASB)

The writer begins by looking at life from a negative perspective. I know that's not popular in today's feel-good, me-centered American Christianity, but it's a good place to start. There is a negative side to godliness; there are things that a godly person just can't do. But this is not about legalism; it's about lordship. And even when we recognize God as the Lord of our lives, our human nature, our flesh, will fight against that. What our spirit knows is right and good is often opposed to what our flesh desires. Although this battle will continue as long as we live, awareness and obedience to God's leadership will ensure our victory in that battle.

When my wife, Terri, and I first started in ministry, we worked with students and youth. During those fifteen years, we were blessed to see God work in the lives of people like you who wanted to go deeper with the Lord.

Three principles I learned from Dr. Jerry Vines became a key to my student ministry. He was speaking about the three young Hebrew men in the fiery furnace, when he made a statement I've never forgotten.

"They wouldn't bow. They wouldn't bend. They wouldn't burn."

Do you remember the story? King Nebuchadnezzar had built a huge golden statue and ordered everyone to bow to it at certain times. But Shadrach, Meshach, and Abednego refused to bow, telling the king that they would worship no god but their own. So as punishment, King Nebuchadnezzar threw them into a fiery furnace—and he was so mad that he had his men heat up the furnace seven times the normal temperature. It was so hot that as the king's soldiers threw the three men into the fire, even the soldiers were burned and killed. But while Shadrach, Meshach, and Abednego were in the furnace, they remained standing. And there appeared to be a fourth man standing with them. Finally, when the furnace was opened again, Shadrach, Meshach, and Abednego walked out unscathed. The Bible says, "not a hair of their heads was singed" (Daniel 3:27). After that, King Nebuchadnezzar became a firm believer in the God of Shadrach, Meshach, and Abednego. He rewarded the three men and declared to everyone else that he would punish anyone who spoke against the God of Shadrach, Meshach, and Abednego.

If we're going to live fireproof lives, we would do well to remember the three principles from that story.

1. They wouldn't bow to the culture. All around us, believers and churches are caving in to the culture, allowing the world to influence the church instead of the church influencing the world. We are no longer salt and light—we're sugar and spice. We cannot allow our lives to be absorbed in stinking thinking. We have to renew our minds daily.

2. They wouldn't bend to the whims of the times. We hear so much today about being politically correct. We can't cater to these demands and remain true to the gospel. There is nothing new under the sun. Sin is still sin, and the cross is still the cross. The Enemy's tactics haven't changed much over the years. Whatever our Enemy and this world's system try to impose on us is usually an attempt to disillusion us into sin.

3. They wouldn't burn under the fires of pressure. They were fireproof. Their beliefs didn't change when they faced the flames of adversity. The goal of the Evil One and those who follow him is to destroy your testimony and your witness. When black and white become a dingy gray, the world feels better about itself. But we are not of this world. We must stand tall with our armor on. The fiery darts are coming.

You and I know what we are *supposed* to do. *Doing* it is the key. Those who think they can get away with living a compromised life—bowing and bending to the demands of the world—are headed for ultimate failure.

When the Israelites took possession of their Promised Land, the land that God had given them, they eventually got tired of fighting the Canaanites. They instead chose a peaceful coexistence. But it didn't work. When you are a child of God, there is no peaceful coexistence with evil. Compromise, loose values, and playing with fire will ultimately get you burned.

James said, "Therefore, submit to God. But resist the Devil, and he will flee from you" (4:7). But we often try to resist without submitting. You can't say no to Satan without first saying yes to God.

When you see someone who calls himself a believer but is continually found walking and talking in the ways of the world, you have to wonder when the fall is going to come.

In the first verse of Psalm 1, notice the progressive nature of sin, the downward spiral toward a wasted life. There are three sets of triplets:

1. **Walk** in the **counsel** of the **wicked**
2. **Stand** in the **path** of **sinners**
3. **Sit** in the **seat** of **scoffers**

When the psalmist refers to our "walk," he is talking about how we make daily decisions based on our worldview. "Stand" refers to our commitment to a particular way of life. And "sit" is a reference to a settled attitude of the heart. It implies total identification. Godly people watch where they go and whom they listen to.

If we desire to be holy and blameless people, we must oppose godless thinking and living. We cannot be found standing in the path of sinners. This refers to a deliberate violation of God's law. The Hebrew word for *sinners* is a picture of someone who makes a loud noise, causes turmoil, or provokes a disturbance. The godly person doesn't make trouble.

In a society that no longer views the laws of God as guidelines for lifestyle, politics, or society in general, it is imperative for the godly to make right choices and stand strong. We have a powerful witness when we are unstained by the world. We can't be the people of God if we have more confidence in *Cosmo* and the Kardashians than in the Word of God. Any principle not based on God's standard will lead you down the path of scoffers.

If you listen to the counsel of the self-willed or imitate the conduct of the self-sufficient or seek the company of scoffers, you will ultimately fail. Listening to them will result in the development of ungodly principles. If you sit around with sarcastic mockers, you'll establish unholy partnerships.

No one becomes ungodly overnight, though. When you see someone falter, it's usually not a blowout. It's a small leak in their soul, some area where they've let their guard down or justified something inexcusable.

A characteristic of scoffers is to blame everyone but themselves for what is wrong in their lives. When confronted by the consequences of their actions, they make excuses. They blame their environment, their heritage, their family, their peers, the computer, or the system—but never themselves.

The "wicked," or the ungodly, are those who live their lives without any thought of God. They have no point of reference in regard to the Lord. But every day believers "ooh" and "ahh" over stars and celebrities and even classmates whose lives are not worth imitating.

A wicked person is not just a mobster or murderer. A wicked person is anyone who does not have time for God in his or her life. Wicked people rule out God in their agenda, their plans, and their relationships. This should sound a fire alarm to believers. If we rule out God by being unfaithful to His laws, by not spending time with Him in His Word and in prayer, wouldn't that also be considered wicked in the eyes of God?

One reason our lives end up in shambles is that we've bought into the lies of the world.

"Look out for #1!"

"I have a right to live how I want!"

"It's okay to bend the rules!"

These are not attitudes of God—these are worldly attitudes that appeal to our human nature, but can wreak havoc in our spiritual lives. The writer of Psalm 1 doesn't fall for it, though. He challenges the "enlightenment" of his present age—as well as our own. He sees people making dead-end choices, and he sees the consequences that result.

You cannot miss the downward spiral here. It begins by someone simply walking along, then hesitating, then standing around to listen. He decides to sit down and take in what he's hearing. It's a lifestyle choice, a decision to hang out with the wrong crowd. Once a person reaches that point, only repentance and removal can save them from tragic failure.

All of us know people who once appeared to walk with God and now care nothing for His ways. At one time they were in youth group every week, but now they couldn't care less about the Word of God. They used to respect the ways of God, but now they mock and scoff at those who are so "narrow-minded."

What happened?

I grew up with a guy who was the greatest soul winner I've ever known. He loved Jesus and lived for Him as a college athlete and ministerial student. But something happened when he went off to seminary. He started to question God's Word. He became too "wise" for the simple truths of Scripture. He received his doctorate but rejected the ways of God and bought into the schemes of the Devil. Today he is out of the ministry and teaching a humanistic worldview at a secular university. What a tragedy—for him and for the Kingdom.

There is an interesting tone to Psalm 1, something you don't often hear in the church today. While the "health-and-wealth" crowd tells us to emphasize the positive, God begins by pointing out the negative. The blessed man is distinguished by the things he doesn't do, the places he refuses to go, the books he will not read, the movies and TV shows he will not watch, and the company he will not keep. Paul reminded the Corinthians, "Do not be deceived: 'Bad company corrupts good morals'" (1 Corinthians 15:33).

Too often believers find themselves in the counsel of the wicked. It is wicked counsel for someone to tell me that I can live life on my own terms and still call myself a follower of Jesus Christ. In fact, living life on my terms not only sets me up to fail, but it is also really nothing more than practicing atheism with a religious façade.

If our lives are going to be fireproof, they have to bear witness that we are strangers and aliens in this world. This world is not our home; this is not where we belong. What difference does it make if you are flying first class by the world's standards when you're on the wrong plane?

> **What difference does it make if you are flying first class when you're on the wrong plane?**

Delight in the Lord

Instead, his delight is in the LORD's instruction,
and he meditates on it day and night. (Psalm 1:2)

Although the first verse of Psalm 1 describes the negative, verse 2 presents the positive side of a blessed life. A person with a fireproof life delights in the Word of God. He meditates on it day and night. When the psalmist refers to the Law, he's not just referring to the Ten Commandments, but to all of God's revelation.

The fireproof life is also characterized by a dependence on the Word. Jeremiah 15:16 says, "Your words were found, and I ate them. Your words became a delight to me and the joy of my heart, for I am called by Your name, Yahweh God of Hosts."

Although I'm not a fan of formulas, I'm going to give you one here:

Love for the Lord

+

Love for His Law

=

A Lifestyle of Godliness

The evidence of a fireproof life is in a person's character. Don't miss this principle: The godly have learned in the hidden, inner parts of their lives to draw on the grace of God.

Fireproof Trees

He is like a tree planted beside streams of water that bears its fruit in season and whose leaf does not wither. Whatever he does prospers. (Psalm 1:3)

The metaphor of trees is common in the Bible—the godly are like trees. When you see a great sequoia you think of strength, steadfastness, and stability. The tree planted by streams of water is symbolic of a life planted in Christ. In Christ, we never worry about a dry season because the River of Life never runs dry. Jesus said, "If you are thirsty, come to Me!" (see John 7:37).

A tree doesn't just stand still. It produces oxygen. It gives shade. And sometimes it nourishes with fruit. Trees support life. They are a shelter in the storm. When I think of the sequoias, I am reminded of what Paul said to the Corinthians: "Therefore, my dear brothers, be steadfast, immovable, always excelling in the Lord's work, knowing that your labor in the Lord is not in vain" (1 Corinthians 15:58).

Fruit is the external evidence of an internal life. Jesus said it simply, "A good tree can't produce bad fruit; neither can a bad tree produce good fruit" (Matthew 7:18). People who are rooted in Christ will produce the fruit of the Spirit: "love, joy, peace, patience, kindness, goodness, faithfulness, gentleness, self-control" (Galatians 5:22–23 NASB). A fruitful tree doesn't just take up space in this world. It produces something that is a benefit and blessing to others.

The psalmist also describes the tree as one "whose leaf does not wither" (Psalm 1:3). It's a symbol of firm consistency to all who see it. In the part of the country where I live, pine trees and evergreens abound. Evergreens are not seasonal; they are steadfast, consistent, continual.

I'm not a botanist, but I do know that dry leaves are the result of dry roots. Often in the South, the heat can be unbearable. If not watered regularly, the trees easily wilt and the leaves wither. The leaf of the tree reflects the condition of the roots.

A fireproof life is a life that is blessed and will bless others. The phrase "whatever he does prospers" in Psalm 1:3 does not refer to material possessions. A man is not necessarily prosperous because he has cars, land, and money. You can have all that and not be blessed. In fact, many who have all the worldly possessions they could ever want are the most miserable people in the world. Nothing satisfies them.

We prosper as our soul prospers. True wealth is not found in the size of an estate or bank account, not in cool cars or cribs, but in sound character and a commitment to laying up treasures in heaven.

The person who has determined to live a fireproof life may have nothing, yet possesses everything. Against that kind of person, the Devil can make little headway.

Satan says, "Serve me, and I'll give you whatever you want."

The fireproof life responds, "I already have everything."

Satan says, "I will take away what you have."

But the believer replies, "You can't, because I don't have anything for you."

Satan may say, "I can take your life!"

To which the Christian responds, "To live is Christ and to die is gain" (Philippians 1:21 NASB).

The heated words of Satan are no match for the fireproof life.

The Wicked in the Wind

Psalm 1 ends with a warning of what happens to the ungodly:

> The wicked are not like this [firmly planted tree];
> instead, they are like chaff that the wind blows
> away. Therefore the wicked will not survive the
> judgment, and sinners will not be in the com-
> munity of the righteous. For the LORD watches
> over the way of the righteous, but the way of the
> wicked leads to ruin. (Psalm 1:4–6)

Everything that was said about the believer earlier in
the psalm is quite the opposite from what is said for the
unbeliever. This psalm is a much-needed reminder that the
world's system will not stand when God sends the fires of
judgment.

Chaff is the dry, scaly flakes that fly off when harvest-
ing grain. It certainly lacks the sturdy stability of a firmly
planted tree. When God begins to sift between the chaff
and the grain, the chaff will not be preserved. It's worthless.
It is easily blown away. And it is highly flammable.

Do you want a fireproof life?

Take a look at Hebrews 11. It can safely be called the
Hall of Fame of the Faithful. If God were rewriting it,
would He consider including you? Are you a person God
would want to write about?

When Paul wrote Second Timothy, he was a prisoner to Nero—the most cruel, vain, inhumane Caesar that had ever led the Roman Empire. Nero commanded all to bow to him and was feared throughout the empire. In contrast, Paul was an obscure Jew who had come to Christ, known only in a few areas of the empire. He spent most of his life being beaten or in prison. Yet today we name our sons Paul and our dogs Nero.

Which would you say had a fireproof life, a fireproof legacy? Paul or Nero?

Several years ago, I had the privilege of attending a pastor's conference with the late Adrian Rogers from Bellevue Baptist Church in Memphis, Tennessee. In a session called "Keeping Pace," Dr. Rogers gave us a bonus: a list of declarations which he used to make sure his life was of use to God. I took notes as fast as I could and have kept them in my prayer notebook ever since. Like me, you may want to write this down so that you can refer to it often.

Praise: I praise God that He has given Himself for me. I praise Him for something new every day. I praise Him for my salvation, redemption, the cross, and indwelling Holy Spirit.

Acceptance: I accept that He has given Himself to me. I accept who I am in Christ. (Just take a concordance and go through the passages in the New Testament where Paul refers to "in Christ" or "with Christ" or "through Christ." It will change the way you think.)

Control: I place myself under the control of God so that He can live His life through me. I give myself to His lordship. I take up my cross. I die daily. It is not I, but Christ.

Expectation: I believe it's going to be a great day as I live my life for God. It's going to be a day where I can be used by God. I make the choice to rejoice.

It takes twenty-one days to start a habit. How about trying to start a new spiritual habit these next twenty-one days? Start each day with these simple yet profound thoughts. Who knows? When the fire comes, you may be able to praise God, accept what's happening, surrender control, and expect God to show you something great in the midst of the fire.

Remember how Psalm 1 ends: "For the LORD watches over the way of the righteous, but the way of the wicked leads to ruin" (v. 6). Choose to walk in the right way, and you will be one step closer to a fireproof life.

Fire Drill!

1. What are some of the ways that you would describe success?

2. Now think about how God may describe a successful life. Are there areas where you need to adjust your ideas to align more closely with God's?

3. Do you have wicked people, sinners, and scoffers in your life? Do you "walk" with them?

4. What does Psalm 1 say about your answer to #3?

5. What kind of fruit is your life producing? How is your life a benefit and blessing to others?

6. What can you do to increase the production of good fruit in your life?

7. What does Psalm 1:6 say is the fate of the wicked? What can you do—today—to ensure that you're on the right path?

CHAPTER 3

A Fireproof Faith

*The genuineness of your faith—more valuable
than gold, which perishes though refined
by fire—may result in praise, glory,
and honor at the revelation of Jesus Christ.*

—1 Peter 1:7

I grew up in a typical Baptist church. We started at eleven o'clock sharp with the prelude and ended at twelve o'clock dull with the benediction. It seemed the pastor never expected God to do anything. No one expected anyone to respond to the invitation. The church, for most of my growing-up years, was dull, dead, and faithless.

Little of faith, discipleship, or commitment was ever mentioned. I recall a lot of hot air but no wind of the Holy Spirit.

Manley Beasley was the greatest man of faith I ever met. Two of his children served on our staff, and we often talked about their dad's faith. Manley's youngest son, Jonathan, once said to me, "The hardest thing about being Dad's son is learning to develop our own faith. When Dad was alive, we depended so much on his faith for us. Now that he's gone, we're having to learn what it means for us personally to walk by faith."

Manley had survived numerous (I'm not exaggerating) incurable diseases. He was as sure as dead more times than anyone can count. He wrote a fantastic workbook on faith that will take you places you've never been. Manley often asked people, "What are you trusting God for today?" Many Christians haven't trusted God for anything since trusting Him for salvation, which is why the saints burn out. They walk by sight, not by faith.

We all want great faith. We just don't want to pay the price. When I saw the faith of Manley Beasley, I wanted it—but to be honest I didn't (and still don't) want to go through the fires he went through to get it.

What Faith Looks Like

Ron Dunn said, "All that believes is not faith, and much of that being called faith today is not faith at all. . . . Any day

now someone is going to sue God for breach of promise."[1]
I would dare say, based on much of what we hear about
faith, many are confused about what biblical faith looks like.
When you listen to the prosperity gospel, faith would seem
to mean a new car, on-the-spot healing, lots of money, and
the repentant return of prodigals. That's not reality. Faith is
not supernatural power on demand.

The other extreme is the failure to believe God altogether. We're told again and again in Scripture that the
"righteous will live by faith" (Romans 1:17; Habakkuk 2:4;
Galatians 3:11, for starters). I came to Christ by faith, and I
continue in Christ by faith.

But what does that mean, exactly? What is faith? How
would we define it from a biblical perspective?

Ron Dunn explained it in three points:

- One, faith is an affirmation. It's our "amen" to all
  God has revealed about Himself.
- Two, it is an act. We obey all that God commands.
- Three, it is an attitude. It is believing that God is
  actively interested and involved in our daily existence.
  And it is this attitude of faith, this resting in Him,
  that God desires.[2]

What do others say when they try to define faith?

> At the end of the day, faith means letting God be
> God. —John Blanchard

Faith is the capacity to trust God while not being able to make sense out of everything. —James Kok

Faith is the sight of the inward eye. —Alexander MacLaren

Faith is the power of putting self aside that God may work unhindered. —F. B. Meyer

Faith is reason at rest in God. —C. H. Spurgeon

Faith does not look at itself. It has no value save as it links us with God. —Vance Havner

Faith is not idle; it works while it waits. —Ron Dunn[3]

Faith is not wishful thinking, presumption, a denial of reality, the power of positive thinking, or positive confession. Faith, according to Hebrews, is "the reality of what is hoped for, the proof of what is not seen" (11:1). As you study the Scriptures, you find that faith is tied to words like *knowing, believing,* and *obeying* the truth. If you don't believe that our God is trustworthy, you'll never be able to walk by faith. The emphasis of the Bible is not on our subjective experiences but on the object of our faith—God Himself.

Mustard-Seed Faith

We are to have faith in God and His Word. In my office, I have a very small jar filled with mustard seeds. Although it is only an inch and a half tall and about a half-inch wide, it contains hundreds of mustard seeds. I bought the jar in Israel as a visible reminder of one of the great teachings of our Lord.

I've often looked at that little jar and wondered, *What could I do if I had faith the size of one of those tiny mustard seeds?* The possibilities are endless. But the embarrassing reality is that most of us fail the tests of faith.

Faith is the starting point on the road to obedience. It is our foundation and sustaining strength in the storms of life. I don't really have faith if I'm not living according to what I say I believe about God and His Word. Too often we can talk a better game than we can live.

Think about just a few of those people from the Bible who were called to put their faith to the test. Remember, they obeyed God in spite of the circumstances or public opinion. They had little rational explanation or physical evidence. They knew that faith, ultimately, rested in knowing and seeing God.

Noah, build an ark.

"Okay, Lord. . . . But what's an ark?"

Abraham, set out for another city.

"What city? Can you toss me down a GPS?"

Abraham, you're going to have a child.

"At my age? Um, do You know how old my wife is?"

Joseph, I've got big plans for you.

"That's great, God, but You're going to have to get me out of this prison first."

Israel, take the land.

"Are You kidding us? We are grasshoppers—they're giants!"

And remember, the Bible records the failures of faith as well.

Peter, get out of the boat.

"And do what? Walk on water?!"

When I think about faith, I am usually reminded of the situation that arose when Jesus talked about mustard-seed faith. Shortly after the Transfiguration (Matthew 17), Jesus, Peter, James, and John were coming down the mountain, and the other disciples were with a man whose son was possessed by a demon. The man had asked the other disciples to deliver the boy, but they couldn't.

After Jesus cast out the demon, the disciples took Jesus aside and asked Him, "Why couldn't we drive it out?" Jesus answered, "Because of your little faith." And that's when Jesus told them, "If you have faith the size of a mustard seed, you will tell this mountain, 'Move from here to there,' and it will move. Nothing will be impossible for you" (Matthew 17:19–20).

Warren Wiersbe writes, "Faith as a grain of mustard seed suggests not only size (God will honor even a little faith), but also life and growth. Faith like a mustard seed is living faith that is nurtured and caused to grow. Faith must be cultivated so that it grows and does even greater things for God (1 Thessalonians 3:10; 2 Thessalonians 1:3). Had the nine disciples been praying, disciplining themselves, and meditating on the Word, they would have been able to cast out the demon and rescue the boy."[4]

If we want God's sustaining power in our lives during difficult times, we need to learn to flex our faith muscles. It's not the size but the object of our faith that matters. Mountain-moving faith is in the power of God.

Mustard-seed faith doesn't see the obstacles; it focuses on our God, who is greater than any obstacle we might face. I can acknowledge that a problem exists, but looking at life through the eyes of faith, the problem is never so big that God is not bigger still. It is His great power, not our great faith, that works in our times of testing. If our test seems mountainous, we need to quit staring at the mountain and focus on the God who created heaven and earth.

The reality is, our faith is going to be tested. We are going to go through the fire. But we are called of God to step out in faith and believe Him. Only then can we be fireproof.

Unbelief

In Psalm 78, we read the words, "They did not believe God or rely on His salvation. . . . They kept sinning and did not believe His wonderful works" (vv. 22, 32). How incredibly strange that God's people, who had seen the hand of God working so mightily on their behalf, would act in such a way. God delivered them from Pharaoh. He made a gushing well of water come out of a rock, and He rained down food from the sky to feed them. But as you read this psalm, you quickly discover their lack of appreciation. In fact, after all of this, they questioned whether God was capable of fulfilling His purpose in their lives. They believed God enough to leave Egypt and get all the way to the edge of the Promised Land, but they lacked the faith to actually step into the Promised Land. At one point God said to Moses, "How long will these people despise Me? How long will they not trust in Me despite all the signs I have performed among them?" (Numbers 14:11).

Instead of walking by faith into all God had promised, they whined in the wilderness. And they died in the wilderness because of their unbelief. They had the Promised Land before them, but they chose to eat dust and bury the dead.

They reached a level of testing where they were unwilling to continue on with God. When we go through the firestorms of life, we have a choice: Do we believe God or do we quit? Will we pass or fail the fire inspection? Faith is a demonstration that the disciples of our Lord refuse to accept failure as final. We know God has the last word.

Far too often we know God's plan, and we've read His Word, but we choose to make our own plans and figure out a fleshly fire escape just in case God doesn't come through. This is a sign of unbelief. We are self-deceived when we try to "help" God or when we think we can handle life's tests and trials on our own.

Faith must fix its attention on the power and promises of God alone. Our strengths are no help to God and our weaknesses no hindrance. Yet, we are slow to trust the Almighty. Rather than resting on His omnipotence, we struggle and wrestle with life in our own strength. What God wants is obedience and the yielding of our will to His.

A. B. Simpson wrote, "The larger the God we know, the larger will be our faith. The secret of power in our lives is to know God and expect great things from Him." If we want to see our faith grow, it has to be tested. God wanted to grow the children of Israel, so He put them to the test.

When was the last time you expected to find God in the fire?

We are to walk by faith, not by sight. Abraham, as the years went by and the promise remained unfulfilled, looked at himself and his wife and said, "No way." The result of his lack of faith was called Ishmael. Rather than waiting on the promise, Abraham and Sarah decided to help God out. Although Abraham is the father of the faithful, he's also the father of a son who was the result of unbelief. As the testing wore on, Abraham became impatient with the Lord. He wasn't getting any younger, you know!

Although Abraham knew the plans and promises of God, he set out to make his own plans. You can read his story of unbelief in Genesis 16. Initially, after God renewed the promise in chapter 15, Abraham believed God. But as time went on, he became impatient. All he had to do was wait for God's timing, but he caved in to his flesh and conceived a child with Hagar. In Abraham's eyes he had planned and gotten what God had promised—a son. But there was a problem: it was not by faith but by the flesh. The unbelief of the father of the faithful caused many heartaches.

The same is true with us. We read the promises. We listen to the sermons. We hear the testimonies of others' faith in God. But then we try to strike out on our own. There's a price to pay for trying to do God's will our own way. Peter reminded us that God has given us "great and precious promises" (2 Peter 1:4). We can't force the promises; we can only trust God to fulfill them in His own time and way.

Passing the Faith Test

Abraham learned from his mistake—we don't see him falter in his faith again. The New Testament presents Abraham as the ultimate illustration of the faith life. Paul told the Romans, "Abraham believed God, and it was credited to him for righteousness" (Romans 4:3). Everything Abraham needed and everything God demanded of him was obtained by faith.

Frank A. Clark said, "A fellow shouldn't abandon his faith when it weakens, any more than he would throw away a suit because it needs pressing."[5] There may be a time when it's hard to find God in your fire, but you can always trust He is there.

When we go through a trial, our faith is being tested. We can talk about faith all we want, but until our faith is tested, we don't know its validity or depth. Until we've thrown ourselves on God's mercy and seen God in the storm, we haven't looked with the eyes of faith. "Our faith is really and truly tested," wrote John Calvin, "only when we are brought into very severe conflicts, and even when hell itself seems opened to swallow us up."[6]

All of us will be tested. All of us will be given a choice to trust our flesh or trust the Father. If you want a fireproof faith, you need to learn some principles from Abraham. After Abraham learned his lesson with Ishmael, God fulfilled His promise with Isaac. Abraham could take some credit for Ishmael, but not for Isaac. What can we learn from this?

1. A fireproof faith has confidence in God. Abraham believed God. The object of faith determines its validity. Abraham no longer trusted in himself but learned to trust the God who makes the impossible possible—the God of creation who makes something out of nothing, the God of the resurrection who makes life out of death.

When you are going through a test of your faith, you have two options: You can fall into the trap of saying, "It's no use; I give up. I've prayed and nothing is happening." Or you can say, "My God is faithful and true. He has never failed to honor His Word. Nothing is impossible with Him." You can choose to cooperate with the omnipotent God of glory. It was said of Abraham, "he believed, hoping against hope" (Romans 4:18). When there was no way, Abraham said, "God has a way." He believed that he might become all God had called him to be.

2. A fireproof faith does not ignore or deny problems. Faith is not living in denial. God made a promise that led Abraham to trust God's word instead of getting caught up in the difficulties. God specializes in problem situations. If He can handle the sin problem, He can handle the saint's problems.

3. A fireproof faith is expressed through confidence in the Word of God. Abraham examined the situation and determined that in spite of his age, in spite of the fact he had failed with Hagar and Ishmael, God could be trusted. The Bible says, the "righteous will live by faith." The Hebrew word for *faith* means firmness or certainty.

4. A fireproof faith must become a way of life. We don't go through just one fire in the Christian life. You are either in the midst of a fire, coming out of one, or headed for one. A fireproof faith is not insurance to escape hell; it's the capacity to live through hell on earth. Abraham did not waver in unbelief. He was more sure of what God said than what his body was telling him as the years passed.

In *Fireproof*, this realization is a turning point for Caleb.

INT. FIRE STATION COMMONS AREA
MICHAEL is standing when CALEB enters.

MICHAEL
You wanted to tell me something?

CALEB
Ah, it's about your faith.

MICHAEL
My faith?

CALEB
Yeah.

MICHAEL
What about it?

CALEB
Well. I'm in.

MICHAEL
You're in?

CALEB
(smiling) Yeah, I'm in.

MICHAEL
Are you saying that you wanna be in?

CALEB
I'm saying, I'm in.

MICHAEL
You're really in?

CALEB
I'm really in.

MICHAEL
'Cause you can't be half in and say you're in.
You gotta be all in, brother.

CALEB
I'm saying, *I'm all in.*

MICHAEL
Oh, Caleb, I can't believe it, man!
You're my brother!

CALEB
I'm your brother?

MICHAEL
Yeah, man, you're my brother from another
mother. But now we've got the same Father!

CALEB
What?

MICHAEL
Aw, I'll explain it to you later,
man. This is awesome.

Caleb's newfound faith is something to celebrate—but not because it's going to make everything easier. It does help him to reprioritize his life, put focus on what really matters, and have hope through the fires.

Faith is the key to the Christian life. Without it, we can't please God. Anything we do apart from faith is sin. Jim Cymbala said, "What is faith? It is total dependence upon God that becomes supernatural in its working."[7]

If I want to fireproof my life, I've got to learn what it means to walk by faith. There is no such thing as a life that can avoid the fires, trials, and storms of life. There is, however, a life that overcomes. It is the life of faith.

Fire Drill!

1. How would you define faith?

2. How would you describe your own faith? As big as a mustard seed?

3. List some of the things that may be possible in your life with a little faith.

4. What are some daily habits you could develop to build your faith?

5. Who are some friends that would or already do support you as you step out in faith?

6. Go back and look at the faith test on pages 45–46. For each item, list at least one example of this in your own life. If you can't think of an example, list one way that you will begin to put this element to work in your life.

CHAPTER 4

Fireproof Your Heart and Mind

*And the peace of God, which surpasses
every thought, will guard your hearts
and minds in Christ Jesus.*

—PHILIPPIANS 4:7

A fireproof life is not a perfect life. If we think it's impossible for us to fail, we deceive ourselves. Remember what Paul said: "Whoever thinks he stands must be careful not to fall" (1 Corinthians 10:12). All of us know someone who doesn't follow that advice. The alarms go off, but they don't heed the warning. One tragic decision can lead to a fallen saint and a tarnished testimony. This is what happens when people do not take seriously the call to put on their armor and stay on their knees.

Some of us don't mature in our character because one part of us frustrates the rest. Our life is stalled in an internal debate. We set out to be all God wants us to be, but the inner battle rages and the mind is filled with contradictions. We give our old nature an audience by arguing with self, rather than doing what we know is right.

In the 1920s and '30s Vance Havner wrote a weekly column for *The Charlotte Observer*. In one article entitled "The Positive Life" the wise prophet wrote:

> Every man has in him positive and negative elements. High thoughts, clean ideals, noble purposes, everything that elevates the tone of life and strengthens its moral fiber is positive. But low and dirty thinking, perverse inclinations, unworthy desires and everything that lowers the moral stamina, weakens the soul's morale, dulls the finer sensibilities and makes the spiritual less real is negative.
>
> What to do with the mixed-up Inside Congress is our problem. If we make a debating society of our inner lives, we get nowhere and our time is frittered away in internal strife. The only way out is to live positively. Decide upon the highest and worthiest course of action, gather all the positive

elements behind it and refuse to give the dissenters the floor.

Any man can tell which are the positives and negatives in his life. Let him give all his time to be positive and the opposition will die from neglect. Let him cultivate wholesome and constructive thinking, helpful friends, good books, uplifting tastes and pursuits and do only those things that build him up. The negative will pop up all along—we cannot help that—but we can refuse to accept, harbor and encourage it.

Particularly in our thought life do we need to discriminate. Negative thoughts are the germs of the spiritual life that infect us with poisons that undermine our integrity and destroy soul-health. Just as in the physical world, some constitutions can throw off these microbes better than others, but none of us can afford to tolerate them for the sturdiest will eventually give way if no action is taken.

All forms of fear, doubt, worry, all morbid, neurotic, unwholesome and vulgar tendencies, all moods, trials and whims that endanger our spiritual vitality must be shunned. When they appear, meet and counteract them with a positive. That is overcoming evil with good.

Do not linger with your Inside Parliament. Vote for the best you know and start doing right to carry the measure through. Hear only affirmation voices and negative will die or line up with you. If you don't, the worst in you will veto the best. The Bible preacher had this in mind when he said, "Whatever things are true, honest, just, pure, lovely, of good report, think on these things."[1]

Wise counsel from a wise man. There is much wisdom in the Bible on how to fireproof your mind and heart. Obviously it is centered on the truth of loving God with all your heart, soul, mind, and strength.

Guard Your Heart

One reason I know the Bible is true is because its standards are high and holy. At the same time, God never tries to gloss over the failures of the heroes of faith. We see them realistically, warts and all. However, that doesn't allow us to make excuses. The examples of their unguarded moments are warnings to us.

When Alexander the Great was at the height of his power, he called in a famous artist to paint his portrait. The painting depicts Alexander with his head in his hands, as if he were thinking. Historians tell us otherwise. Alexander had a horrible scar on one cheek and was so ashamed that he hid the scar as he posed for the portrait.

The Holy Spirit does not hide the scars of the saints. They are in the Word for our teaching, reproof, correction, and training in righteousness.

"Now these things became examples for us, so that we will not desire evil things . . . they were written as a warning to us" (1 Corinthians 10:6, 11). Paul reminded the believers in Corinth, and us, that just because we have strong faith doesn't mean we are immune from fiery darts or our own flesh. Paul used Israel as an example to believers, lest we fall into the same traps.

Paul exhorted the Corinthians to live lives of self-discipline. Life is a battle with the world, the flesh, and the Devil. We face persecution and temptation that can burn us if we aren't on guard. If our lives are going to stand up to the fire, we can't live as we please.

The Israelites experienced a powerful deliverance from Egypt, but it didn't take them long to forget. Look at their advantages: They had a godly leader in Moses, they saw great miracles, and they had guidance from a great God. God brought them out of Egypt through the Red Sea, but they still turned away. They doubted and complained and, as a result, most of them never made it to the Promised Land.

The Israelites were set free, but areas of their lives were unguarded. They did not guard their hearts, and their testimonies were burned by idolatry, sexual immorality, testing God, and complaining. In each situation the consequences were death. When we fail to learn from their bad examples, we can make the same mistakes.

The reason we need to fireproof our lives is that we are all idolaters at heart. Paul identified coveting as idolatry (see

Colossians 3:5). We make popularity, power, and possessions our gods.

According to the *Evangelical Dictionary of Biblical Theology*,

> The testimony of Scripture is that God alone is
> worthy of worship. Active acknowledgment of
> idols by prostration sacrifice, or other means of
> exaltation is not only a misdirection of allegiance;
> it robs God of the glory and honor that is right-
> fully his (Isaiah 42:8). . . . The sense of Scrip-
> ture was to destroy idolatry or be destroyed by
> it. Since idolatry presented an alternative world
> view, the pressure to worship idols was felt in all
> aspects of life. Social idolatry became a family
> affair, involving cities, towns, clans, and tribes.[2]

Idolatry is a heart issue. In the New Testament it is
associated with pride, self-centeredness, greed, and gluttony. We can't read the Scriptures without seeing repeated
warnings regarding idols. Idolatry is contrary to a Christian
worldview. It is an attempt to offer an explanation for life
apart from God's sovereignty.

Idolatry is also a head issue. When we begin to covet or
love something other than God in the heart, the mind goes
places it should not go and leads to dangerous choices. We
take risks we can't afford.

There are three people in you today: the person you are,
the person you could be for God, and the person you could
become if you let Satan get a foothold in your life. God sees

the heart, and He knows our mind. We can lie to our friends and even try to lie to ourselves. But deep down inside we know when we are leaving a door open for the Enemy. "For who among men knows the thoughts of a man except the spirit of the man that is in him?" (1 Corinthians 2:11).

In the movie *Fireproof*, Caleb Holt struggles with pornography. In one scene his wife Catherine walks in and asks him, "Did you clear your history?" referring to erasing the history on his computer to hide the websites he's been viewing. He tries to play dumb, but in reality his mind and heart have been lured into Internet porn. It affects his thoughts, his affection, and his ability to understand what true love is all about. When confronted, he immediately becomes defensive. Only when he surrenders his life to Christ is he able to smash (quite literally) his computer problem.

I've heard it said that no one becomes involved in adultery, sexual abuse, or homosexuality who has not first been affected by pornography. When I was young, you'd have to go to the store and buy a magazine, but that has changed completely. Now it's so easily accessible, you barely even have to sneak. It's on your phone, everywhere you go, right there in the palm of your hand.

But God knew these days were coming, and the solution is as simple and timeless as it always was. James said, "Therefore, submit to God. But resist the Devil, and he will flee from you" (James 4:7). Okay, I said, "simple," but not easy. We're all guilty of trying to resist without submitting. But when we begin by submitting to God, the resisting becomes so much easier when we're tempted. Sexual sin begins in the mind before it ever plays out in our actions. Sin is birthed in our minds, takes root in our hearts, and ultimately bursts forth to destroy our lives. But by resisting from the start, we gain our footing and can hold strong against sin.

When I was a youth minister, I had two rules for youth camp:

1. Be where you are supposed to be, when you are supposed to be there, doing what you are supposed to be doing.
2. When in doubt, don't.

I told the kids if they would follow those rules, they would never get in trouble. Those same rules apply to us when it comes to fireproofing our hearts and minds.

Reaping the Consequences

The example of Israel is obvious. Paul uses it like a hammer to drive a pin into the inflated balloon of pride. Israel didn't do what they were told. When Moses was on the mountain meeting with God, they were in the valley dancing in the sand. Because Israel did not obey, they forfeited their right to the Promised Land for forty years. That's quite a price to pay for doing things their own way. They thought they knew better than God, so their hearts turned to worship a golden calf. They were overcome with fear of the giants in the land, and they turned away from taking God's promised inheritance. At every turn the Israelites are examples of how not to live the life of faith. They were tested and they failed.

Another example is David. With a single glance David began a downward spiral that almost destroyed him. One glance led to an act of adultery and then to a murder plot. He spent a year trying to cover up what he had done, but it ate away at his body and soul.

David was at the peak of his power and influence when he fell. At the time when kings were supposed to be going to war, David stayed in Jerusalem. The Bible says, "One evening David got up from his bed and strolled around on the roof of the palace" (2 Samuel 11:2). He was being lazy and it led to lust. If he had been where he was supposed to be, when he was supposed to be there, doing what he was supposed to be doing, he wouldn't have fallen into the trap set for him.

Lazy moments need to be feared more than hard labor. One misstep when you aren't spiritually sharp can ruin a reputation for a lifetime. An idle brain is the Devil's workshop. Thomas Brooks wrote, "Idleness is the very source of sin." The great prayer warrior E. M. Bounds said, "Our laziness after God is our crying sin. . . . No man gets God who does not follow hard after him." David grew lazy. He was probably middle-aged around this time. He had survived Saul's persecution and many other battles and had established his kingdom. Maybe he just decided to take a break, to chill out. After all, he had "earned" it.

Our idle days can become Satan's busiest days. It seems the Enemy is always looking for an opportunity to work the most when we want to do the least. Richard Baxter said, "Laziness breeds a love of amusement."

From his roof David saw Bathsheba bathing. Maybe he couldn't have avoided the first glance, but the stare was inexcusable. Our minds are like an airport runway—we can choose what we allow to land there. David's look turned to lust. He was careless with his thoughts, and it resulted in a carnal act. When you read 2 Samuel 11, you see the progression. He saw her, he sent for her, and he slept with her.

David's sin was not merely an isolated act of adultery. His lustful actions led to a pregnancy, which ultimately led David to murder. On the downward spiral of an unguarded heart and mind, David plotted the death of a trusted and loyal soldier. One of the Devil's lies is that we'll be satisfied if we fulfill a passion or appetite in a biblically inconsistent way. The very opposite is true: The more we feed the passion inappropriately, the more it grows and can't be fulfilled.

We know the effects of David's sin when we read his words in Psalm 32:3–4: "When I kept silent [about my sin], my bones became brittle from my groaning all day long. For day and night Your hand was heavy on me; my strength was drained as in the summer's heat." It closes with "Selah," which means, "to pause and think about it." We are told to meditate on what's been said. Maybe Solomon had his own father in mind when he wrote Proverbs 28:13, "The one who conceals his sins will not prosper, but whoever confesses and renounces them will find mercy."

When God saved us, He didn't remove our capacity to sin. He did put His Spirit within us to convict us of sin. Falling down in a pool of water won't cause you to drown, but lying face down in it will. David felt the heavy hand of God on his life and finally surrendered to God in humility and brokenness.

People who make no effort to fireproof their minds and hearts end up doing one of three things:

1. They *rationalize*. They buy the lie of this world's system and refuse to call sin what it is. They refuse to agree with God.
2. They *get busy* and try to ignore the problem, wearing a mask and becoming hypocrites. But busyness can't cover up a barren life.
3. They *compare their sin* to someone else's. They say, "I may have a problem, but I know people who are worse than I am." Making excuses and pointing fingers will only lead you down a path where your testimony will go up in smoke.

If we put off repenting another day, we have one more day to repent of and one less day to repent in. We need to be quick to respond to the convicting power and prompting of the Holy Spirit. Sometimes He will use the Word; sometimes He will use the loving rebuke of a brother or sister in

Christ, like Nathan with David. Rather than playing games, we need to be quick to confess.

The Christ Life: Our Strength

The key to what people see of our lives is the inner life they don't see. "Set your minds on what is above, not on what is on the earth. For you have died, and your life is hidden with the Messiah in God" (Colossians 3:2–3). Simply put, Christ's life was hidden in God. Our lives can be identified with His and share the same hiding place.

I doubt if anyone reading these pages hasn't longed for a life this world could not touch, worry, harass, damage, or destroy. We desire to move through all the traps of trouble without fear or harm. Who wouldn't want an untouchable life, one beyond the reach of the fiery darts of the Enemy?

Jesus alone lived that kind of life. He moved through an antagonistic world and faced hostility, but it never moved Him. How did He do it? He had identified Himself with God the Father. You can't kill life. You can tear up the form it assumes or crucify the body it uses, but life itself can't be touched.

Incorporating Christ as our life sounds mystical. It is, in fact, very practical and possible. Our life can be hidden with Christ in God. Christ makes the thought a reality because He first lived that life for us. The last Adam empowers us to live as the first Adam never could. Because our lives are in Christ, with Christ, and through Christ, we have victory.

Most believers who get burned have failed to understand basic truths about life in Christ. Allowing our minds to drift from heavenly realities produces spiritually bankrupt lives. In his letter to the Romans, Paul wrote:

> So, you too consider yourselves dead to sin but alive to God in Christ Jesus. Therefore do not let sin reign in your mortal body, so that you obey its desires. And do not offer any parts of it to sin as weapons for unrighteousness. But as those who are alive from the dead, offer yourselves to God, and all the parts of yourselves to God as weapons for righteousness. For sin will not rule over you, because you are not under law but under grace. What then? Should we sin because we are not under law but under grace? Absolutely not! (Romans 6:11–15)

In Colossians 3 Paul speaks of being with Christ to show us the sufficiency of our Savior. We must fill our minds with the Word of God and our hearts with His love, or we will fail to pursue the fullness of Christ. Paul tells us to "set" our minds, or think thoroughly about this. This is to be our inner disposition. J. B. Lightfoot paraphrases Paul's words with the following: "You must not only seek heaven, you must also think heaven."[3]

We have died. It happened the moment we were saved. The penalty and price of sin has been paid by our Defender, who lives within us. And that Presence within us is greater than he that is in the world. We are still aware of the presence and power of sin, but no longer condemned or controlled by it. We are hidden with Christ in God and now you may "share in the divine nature" (2 Peter 1:4).

Warren Wiersbe further expounds on our death with Christ: "The fullest explanation of this wonderful truth is found in Romans 6–8. Christ not only died for us (substitution), but we died with Him (identification). Christ not only died for sin, bearing its penalty; but He died unto sin, breaking its power. We are dead and alive at the same time—dead to sin and alive in Christ."[4]

The possibility can be reality. The hidden life makes it possible for the revealed life to be victorious. My life is fireproof when I understand that the world cannot reach my hidden, true source for living because God is my life.

We can be harassed, though. The fiery darts will come. But if we are hidden with Christ in God, we are overcomers through Christ our Lord. Dr. A. T. Robertson wrote, "So here we are in Christ who is in God, and no burglar, not even Satan himself, can separate us from the love of God in Christ Jesus."[5]

Romans 8 holds a beautiful reminder to us that our lives are fireproof in Christ:

> If God is for us, who is against us? He did not even spare His own Son but offered Him up for us all; how will He not also with Him grant us everything? Who can bring an accusation against God's elect? God is the One who justifies. Who is the one

who condemns? Christ Jesus is the One who died, but even more, has been raised; He also is at the right hand of God and intercedes for us. Who can separate us from the love of Christ? (vv. 31–35)

God is on our side, without a doubt. So, how can we make sure that we stay on His side, aligning our hearts with His? These questions can serve as a regular checkup as you spend time alone with the Lord and align your heart and mind with His.[6]

- Am I pure in heart? Are my motives pure? Have I laid down allegiances and affections I have cherished more than Jesus? Do I have single-minded devotion to Jesus Christ? (Matthew 5:8; 2 Corinthians 11:3)
- Is my righteousness merely external, like that of the Pharisees, or does it come from my heart? (Matthew 5:20; 22:36–38)
- Do I have anything that is a master to me besides the Lord Jesus Christ? Am I holding on to anything that is causing me to treat Christ lightly or give Him less than His rightful place? (Matthew 6:24)
- Am I consistently in a position to hear the Word of God? Am I listening intently to God's voice to me, or am I merely paying casual attention? (Matthew 7:24)
- Am I actively and immediately obeying God as He speaks to my heart through His Word? (Matthew 7:24–27)

As you continue to examine your heart and mind, making a continual effort to strengthen your life in Christ and against the forces of this world, you will notice a changed perspective, easier obedience, a greater joy, and a soul that will withstand the fires of life.

Fire Drill!

1. Name some modern-day idols that you've seen people worship today.

2. Do you have any idols in your own life? List them now. (Be honest with yourself so that you can move them out of your life and grow closer to God.)

3. When have you been lazy in guarding your heart? What were the consequences?

4. What are some steps you can take now to guard your heart and mind? What are the benefits of each one?

5. What does being "in Christ" or "with Christ" mean for you? How does this change the way you look at the fires of life?

6. Take a few minutes to write down the checkup questions on page 65. Put them in a journal, in your Bible, or hang them on your mirror where you'll see them regularly. Give your heart and mind regular checkups so that you're healthy and strong for the firestorms ahead.

CHAPTER 5

Fireproof Convictions

God is faithful, and He will not allow you
to be tempted beyond what you are able,
but with the temptation He will also provide
a way of escape so that you are able to bear it.

—1 Corinthians 10:13

One key to having a fireproof life is knowing how to survive the onslaught of Satan. We are in a battle, and attacks will come. Hardly a day goes by without hearing of someone who has stumbled and fallen in the faith. And when our own lives start running at such a frantic pace that we run ahead of our character development, we quickly find ourselves in a danger zone. Living in the fast lane can make compromise look appealing, but there's also more damage when you crash.

In a survey by *Discipleship Journal* some years ago, readers were asked to list their strongest temptations. In order of priority, the "top ten" were:

- Materialism
- Pride
- Self-Centeredness
- Laziness
- Anger/Bitterness (tie)
- Sexual Lust
- Envy
- Gluttony
- Lying

Of those surveyed, 81 percent said they were more likely to yield to temptation when they neglected their time alone with God; 57 percent said they were more likely to yield when they were physically tired.[1]

We all face these temptations. At times I've let anger get a foothold. I've been in situations where I was wronged and could have easily allowed bitterness to take root in my life.

Some days I've been lazy in my pursuit of God. I've been jealous of others and envied their positions. I have faced the temptation to lust. Jesus was so clear on the subject of lust and mental adultery that no man can claim to be exempt.

Materialism has tempted us all. How many times have you wanted something you didn't need and promised to mow the yard for the rest of your life to get it? After all, we must have the newest, latest gadget to keep up with our friends. The problem is, our friends are also trying to keep up with us.

When confronted with these enticements, who hasn't been tempted to lie? We lie to cover our tracks. We lie to impress people. We lie to our friends. We sing songs in church that are not true of our lives. We say that we believe the Word, yet don't do what it says. Again, we lie.

I have a pastor friend whose father, also a pastor, had an affair. He said to his son, "Sundays are the hardest days of my life. I was born to preach and now I can't. I blew it because I cared about my flesh more than my faith."

And although we won't all grow up to be pastors, surely we can identify with that last statement.

Temptation's Realities

Temptation is an invitation to do the wrong thing—or even to do the right thing in the wrong way. Sin is the willingness to act on that temptation. The biggest problem we face is not *knowing* what is right, but *being willing* to do what is right. Most of us have preset convictions on a variety of subjects. But how do we fireproof these convictions so they'll stand up under the weight of temptation?

Matthew's Gospel records the account of Jesus' own dealings with temptation.

Then Jesus was led up by the Spirit into the wilderness to be tempted by the Devil. After He had fasted 40 days and 40 nights, He was hungry. Then the tempter approached Him and said, "If You are the Son of God, tell these stones to become bread." But He answered, "It is written: Man must not live on bread alone but on every word that comes from the mouth of God." Then the Devil took Him to the holy city, had Him stand on the pinnacle of the temple, and said to Him, "If You are the Son of God, throw Yourself down. For it is written: He will give His angels orders concerning you, and they will support you with their hands so that you will not strike your foot against a stone." Jesus told him, "It is also written: Do not test the Lord your God." Again, the Devil took Him to a very high mountain and showed Him all the kingdoms of the world and their splendor. And he said to Him, "I will give You all these things if You will fall down and worship me." Then Jesus told him, "Go away, Satan! For it is written: Worship the Lord your God, and serve only Him." Then the Devil left Him, and immediately angels came and began to serve Him. (Matthew 4:1–11)

First, let's establish some facts about temptation. **Temptation exists because we have a tempter.** He's not a medieval character dressed in red with a pitchfork. He is the Prince of Darkness, the Accuser of the Brethren, and he is in rebellion against God.

Temptation is real and inevitable. You will be tempted, but the temptation itself is not sin. If Lucifer tempted the sinless Son of God, then he is going to come after you—and you don't have to feel guilty about it!

Temptation often comes when we least expect it. Adam and Eve fell in the garden. Abraham shrank back on his walk of faith when he lied to the pharaoh. Elijah caved into discouragement and fear right after his victory on Mt. Carmel.

Temptation can come in the area of your strength. Your strengths can become your weakness. Remember, your talents and abilities are no help to God in empowering you to resist the Devil.

Temptation is allowed by God. The Spirit compelled Jesus to go out to the wilderness. The reality is this: until your faith has been tested, it hasn't been proven.

Temptation never stops. "After the Devil had finished every temptation, he departed from Him for a time" (Luke 4:13). The Devil wasn't through trying, but he had exhausted his options at that point. Satan retreats in order to regroup.

Jesus was "led up by the Spirit into the wilderness." To the Jews of the first century, the wilderness had both a good and bad reputation. The bad reputation was that the wilderness was associated with demons (see, for example, Luke 11:24). The good reputation was that the wilderness was a place of spiritual retreat—a place where Moses, Abraham, and the prophets went to escape the world's pressures and meet God in intimate fellowship. In the wilderness you're either going to meet God in a significant way or be overpowered by the Devil and give up.

In the wilderness of temptation there is both the possibility of strengthening and the potential for seduction. James gives us the order: "Therefore, submit to God. But resist the Devil, and he will flee from you" (4:7). We can't resist if we don't first submit.

Though temptation may take many subtle forms, Satan has three predictable methods of attack, which John summarized as "the lust of the flesh, the lust of the eyes, and the pride in one's lifestyle" (1 John 2:16). These are the same tactics he used in the Garden of Eden, and they have proven successful for centuries. (The Devil may be crafty, but he's not very creative!)

The Lust of the Flesh

First, Satan appeals to our flesh:

> The woman said to the serpent, "We may eat the fruit from the trees in the garden. But about the fruit of the tree in the middle of the garden, God said, 'You must not eat it or touch it, or you will die.'"

"No! You will not die," the serpent said to the woman. "In fact, God knows that when you eat it your eyes will be opened and you will be like God, knowing good and evil." (Genesis 3:2–5)

Satan lured Eve into sin by saying, "You have a right to be happy. You deserve more than you are getting. Since God made you like this, there's nothing wrong with satisfying your desires." To Jesus he said, "If You are the Son of God, and since You've been without food for forty days, why not tell these stones to become bread?" Think about it—if Moses could speak to a rock and see water come forth, surely the Son of God could turn stones to bread. Satan whispers, "You've got the desire, the need, and the ability. Go ahead and satisfy the longings of your flesh."

When Satan made a demand on the deity of Christ, Christ responded as a man. "Man shall not live by bread alone." Jesus didn't overcome the appeal to His flesh on the basis of His deity, but on the basis of His humanity. He never used His power for His own benefit. He submitted Himself to the Word of God, not to the rumbling in His stomach.

Satan entices us to give in to our cravings and let our physical appetites dictate how we live. The key was not in Jesus quoting Scripture. You can quote Scripture while eating your fifth jelly doughnut. The key is submitting your human desires to the authority of Scripture. The Devil has a shallow view of man. He wants us to live on a shallow level. He tempts us to live according to our five senses. He knows that if you think life is to be found in living it up, you'll do everything in your power to please your flesh. But if you believe God's Word and know Christ as your sufficiency, you'll be able to stand on the authority of His Word, just as Jesus did.

While the children of Israel were in the wilderness, God miraculously spared them by providing manna from heaven. "He humbled you and let you be hungry, and fed you with manna which you did not know, nor did your fathers know, that He might make you understand that man does not live by bread alone, but man lives by everything that proceeds out of the mouth of the LORD" (Deuteronomy 8:3 NASB). Unfortunately they became ungrateful, murmuring, and criticizing. Chuck Swindoll points out that when everything seems to be going well, you can expect surprise attacks from the Enemy.

> We get our theological ducks in a row, we make sure our eternal destination is sealed in a fireproof safe, we surround ourselves with a predictable schedule that protects us from contamination with the lost world, and then, like a 600-pound grizzly, we settle down for a long winter's snooze.
>
> Our hope? Do not disturb 'til the Rapture. And we're content to spend the balance of our lives as unconcerned and uninvolved in our world as a silverfish crawling over a pile of discarded *Time* magazines. Only one problem. The battle continues to rage, no matter what the season.

From spring to summer. In relaxed autumn and icy winter. Whether we choose to believe it or not.

It is so easy to forget that our adversary, like our Advocate, neither slumbers nor sleeps. With relentless, unslacking energy . . . as sure as this morning's dawn, he's on the prowl, "seeking someone to devour" (1 Peter 5:8).

He's been at it for centuries. By means of a brilliant strategy, an insidious scheme, he takes advantage of our mental dullness. Surprise attacks are his specialty.

Small wonder Jesus kept urging His followers to "be on the alert," to "watch," to "resist," to keep a clean crop, free of stuff that "chokes the word, making it unfruitful."

Why? Because you never know when you are in the crosshairs of the scope of the Enemy's high-powered rifle. It could be today that you will be the target. When you least expect it . . . in the lazy days of summer, in the cool days of autumn, in the fog of false security, under the frost of a laid-back lifestyle.

He's looking for you. He's primed and ready to fire. And he doesn't wait for hunting season. In fact, as far as Satan is concerned, it's always open season on Christians.

Are you alert to the danger?[2]

The Lust of the Eyes

Satan's second method of attack is by appealing to our eyes:

> So he took Him up and showed Him all the king-
> doms of the world in a moment of time. The Devil
> said to Him, "I will give You their splendor and
> all this authority, because it has been given over
> to me, and I can give it to anyone I want. If You,
> then, will worship me, all will be Yours." And Jesus
> answered him, "It is written: Worship the Lord
> your God, and serve Him only." (Luke 4:5–8)

Perhaps Satan transported Jesus to the mountains of Moab where He could see the caravans moving along the great trade routes from all the nations of the known world. As Satan showed Jesus the kingdoms of the world and all their glory, he was offering the Son of Man a political messiahship. It's what the Jews were expecting. It's what they wanted. So Satan baited Him: "Go ahead, Jesus, give them what they want. Accommodate Your message to the expectations of the people."

The irony of it all is that as God's Son, Jesus had a divine right to all the kingdoms of the world—and at the end of time, He will take His rightful place on the throne. Satan was simply suggesting that Jesus circumvent the Father's timetable.

So Satan appealed to the lust of the eyes. "Jesus, do You like what You see? Don't You wish You had control of all that? I can give it to You. You don't have to go to the cross. You don't have to suffer. Why wait for what You can have now? Why submit to being a servant when You can reign as King now? I am merely offering You a shortcut to what Your Father has already promised You."

Satan wasn't offering Jesus something he didn't have—this temptation was no bluff. The Devil is the god of this age and the head of this world's system. "We know that we are of God, and the whole world is under the sway of the evil one" (1 John 5:19). This offer was consistent with Satan's methods of enticing Eve, David, and others down through the centuries. The Enemy appealed to delights, desires, and pleasures. "Take a look. What do You think? It's all Yours if You will worship me. You can cut a few corners to satisfy Your desires. Just kiss my ring and bow at my feet."

The true nature of this temptation is found in the original language of Luke 4:5–6. The phrase "in a moment of time" is derived from the Greek word *stigma*, the same word used to describe the beatings Christ would receive. The phrase "because it has been given over to me" is the same wording used when Jesus was "given" to be crucified (see Matthew 26:45).

So here's the crux of the temptation: "Jesus, You can have the glory without the cross. No stigma, no betrayal, no being handed over. You can have all the gain with none of the pain."

But there was a price tag attached. Satan was not inviting Jesus to abandon His mission altogether, but to fulfill it in another way. He tempted the Lord to compromise in order to accomplish the plan. The lust of the eyes is always looking for ways to fulfill life on our terms with as little discomfort and sacrifice as possible.

Have you ever been tempted to compromise? Think about something you've really wanted—a car, certain clothes, another person. The Devil will tell you, "I can get that for you. I can arrange that. Just one thing—you'll have to hand over control of your life to me."

The Enemy won't ask you to abandon your faith, but he will compel you to compromise, cut corners, and water down your faith. He will assure you of no pain and all gain, but his promises are empty. He can't give you anything that lasts.

What if he offers you fame, for instance? Andy Warhol said we all get fifteen minutes of fame, but I think he was overestimating. Can you remember who won the Super Bowl or the World Series last year? How about the winners of the Academy Awards five years ago? John's admonition rings true to this day: "And the world with its lust is passing away, but the one who does God's will remains forever" (1 John 2:17).

We are all tempted to cut corners in our efforts to climb the ladder of success. We have all wanted to be the "big man on campus" or the homecoming queen. Someone asked

Chuck Colson why anyone would want to be president of the United States. Colson answered with one word: "POWER!" The seed of Satan's rebellion was birthed in a desire to control. He wants to run the show. Years ago I wrote down these points in my Bible that describe our adversary:

- His master passion is found in Isaiah 14:14—to be "like the Most High."
- His master perversion is found in Genesis 3:5—"you will be like God."
- His main desire is found in Luke 4:7—"worship me."
- His main motive is found in 2 Thessalonians 2:4— "He opposes and exalts himself above every so-called god or object of worship, so that he sits in God's sanctuary, publicizing that he himself is God."

Whatever you worship, you will ultimately serve. Jesus declared to the Devil His intention to worship His heavenly Father and serve Him only. He refused to cut corners. He was here to change the eternal destiny of the human race for all time. The Father had a game plan, and Christ would one day rule over the kingdoms of the world, at the appointed time. Being eternal, Jesus wasn't in a hurry.

If you want to overcome the lust of the eyes, make some decisions right now. First, make a decision about sin (see Romans 6:2). Next, make a decision about your goals in life (see Philippians 1:21). Finally, make a decision about your allegiance (see Romans 6:11–14).

In *Fireproof*, when Caleb finally made a decision against temptation, he got serious. When the flashing ad with a beautiful young girl called to him from the computer, he took the computer, monitor and all, and headed outside. After placing the computer on an outdoor table, Caleb picked up an aluminum bat and smashed the computer and the temptation it held. Out of context, that may seem extreme, but that little box in Caleb's living room was ruining his life, and Caleb finally got serious enough to make sure the temptation had no more power over him.

The Pride of Life

Finally, Satan appeals to our pride. When Satan comes at Jesus for the knockout punch, he doesn't hesitate.

> So he took Him to Jerusalem, had Him stand on the pinnacle of the temple, and said to Him, "If You are the Son of God, throw Yourself down from here. For it is written: He will give His angels orders concerning you, to protect you, and they will support you with their hands, so that you will not strike your foot against a stone." And Jesus answered him, "It is said: Do not test the Lord your God." After the Devil had finished every temptation, he departed from Him for a time. (Luke 4:9–13)

Satan is relentless as he increases the pressure. Don't overlook where he took our Lord—to the heart of the nation, Jerusalem; to the heart of the city, the temple; to the highest point of the temple, the pinnacle. Jesus loved Jerusalem, and Satan knew that. Jesus would minister in the streets, perform miracles, and weep over its people. The temptation was simple: "Since it's only a matter of time before You start Your miracle-working business, why not start now?"

The Devil pulled out Psalm 91, knowing the verses would resonate with Christ, "For He will give His angels orders concerning you, to protect you in all your ways. They will support you with their hands so that you will not strike your foot against a stone" (vv. 11–12). Here's the Devil's subtle twist: since Jesus was going to live by the Word of God, He should be confronted by the Word of God. Satan put Jesus to a Bible test. "If You won't use Your miraculous powers to help Yourself, at least let Your Father show You how much He loves You. Let Him reveal His power on Your behalf. Go ahead, Jesus, jump off the temple. Your Father won't let You fall."

The temptation was to do something dramatic and heroic. Even in the eyes of the most skeptical Jews, this would have been proof that Jesus was the Messiah. So Satan prods Him: "Aren't You willing to take God at His word? Throw Yourself down. Prove to all Israel that You are the Promised One. Prove that Your Father can be trusted."

Isn't it true that we are in awe of the spectacular? We love big shows, big events, big fireworks, and big concerts. The bigger, the better.

This is the "pride in one's lifestyle."

G. Campbell Morgan wrote, "It is when we doubt a person that we make experiments to discover how far they are to be trusted." To test God is to doubt Him. To doubt God is to disbelieve Him. And unbelief is sin.

Jesus refused to abuse His Father's power to attract a crowd. In the wilderness, man is put to the test, not God. Jesus refused to be a sanctified stunt-

> **To test God is to doubt Him.**

man. He didn't come to prove Himself by walking on hot coals, putting His head in the lion's mouth, or leaping tall buildings in a single bound.

In reality the appeal to our pride is a temptation to test God. This is what the children of Israel did—they put God to the test (see Deuteronomy 6:16). They were blessed, protected, and fed, but they complained and bellyached about their conditions.

We are guilty of testing God when we use the Bible to make demands of God, as Satan attempted to do with Jesus. God honors His Word, but He does not misuse or abuse it. Scripture is not a magic wand for us to wave on a whim. Satan quoted some verses from Psalm 91, but he left out verse 14: "Because he is lovingly devoted to Me, I will deliver him; I will protect him because he knows My name."

God will not bless us or deliver us because we spew out a few verses. God's power is for those who love Him, not those who manipulate Scripture to puff themselves up.

The Bible is full of admonitions about pride:

- "To fear the LORD is to hate evil. I hate arrogant pride, evil conduct, and perverse speech." (Proverbs 8:13)
- "Everyone with a proud heart is detestable to the LORD; be assured, he will not go unpunished." (Proverbs 16:5)
- "Pride comes before destruction, and an arrogant spirit before a fall." (Proverbs 16:18)
- "But He gives greater grace. Therefore He says: God resists the proud, but gives grace to the humble." (James 4:6)

Pride is the opposite of humility. Jesus approached His wilderness temptations with two things: the Spirit of God and a mind filled with the Word of God. He never used His position as the Son of God to overcome Satan. He used the same tools that are available to us: the Spirit and the Word.

So how can you develop that same strength to withstand the fires of temptation?

Be on guard. Learn the schemes of the Devil. There are no new tricks in his bag, and he plays his trump card early. He is possessed by lust and pride, so keep your armor on.

Be prepared. Jesus knew the Word. He didn't have to run to church to get the preacher's advice. And He didn't just quote Scripture; He lived it. His reactions reflect more than passing a Scripture memory class. He was obviously immersed in the Word.

Be discerning. Don't be naïve. Don't say, "I will never do that." "That will never happen to me." Remember, "So, whoever thinks he stands must be careful not to fall" (1 Corinthians 10:12).

The story is told of a revolution in which the heir to the throne was taken hostage by the mobs. They thought they could torture him and tempt him to renounce his kingship. They placed him with the foulest people in the country and tried to destroy his character. Yet with each temptation and each prodding to do evil, he would stomp his feet and shout, "No! No! No! I was born to be a king!"

YOU are a child of the King. Don't let the world, your flesh, or the Devil tell you any differently.

Fire Drill!

1. The survey at the beginning of the chapter said, "Eighty-one percent said they were more likely to yield to temptation when they neglected their time alone with God; 57 percent said they were more likely to yield when they were physically tired." Based on those statistics, what are two simple ways to avoid temptation?

2. What are some ways that you have been tempted?

3. Were these temptations either "the lust of the flesh, the lust of the eyes, and the pride in one's lifestyle" as listed in 1 John 2:16?

4. Did you act on those temptations? What was the result?

5. Think about the one temptation that you face most often. How do you think Jesus would respond if Satan tempted Him in the same way? Spend some time in your Bible finding just the right response for that temptation.

CHAPTER 6

Fireproof Decision-Making

Trust in the LORD with all your heart,
and do not rely on your own understanding;
think about Him in all your ways,
and He will guide you on the right paths.

—PROVERBS 3:5–6

When faced with a big decision, what's your process for choosing which way to go? How do you *know* you'll make the right choice?

My wife, Terri, is a great teacher and very discerning. While teaching one group, she told them it concerns her when she hears a Christian say, "Well, I have a peace about it," or, "It all worked out smoothly, so it must have been God's will."

That, of course, is not necessarily the case. God's will does not always take us down an easy road. We can't have the peace of God if we aren't obedient to the will and the Word of God. Any peace we experience apart from obedience is a false sense of security that comes from, frankly, lying to ourselves.

During my senior year of college, I was trying to decide where to attend seminary, and a friend suggested that I visit Midwestern Seminary in Kansas City. One weekend Terri and I and another couple drove through the night to Midwestern. We enjoyed our time there and met some wonderful people. We believed God was leading us to Kansas City.

Our decision made no sense, however, to a lot of people, especially our families. Midwestern was over twenty hours from home and family, and we only knew one couple there. We would have to pay for it ourselves without any outside financial assistance. People thought we were crazy, and we probably were. New Orleans Baptist Theological Seminary offered me a full scholarship, but I didn't believe that was God's plan for us. It would have been the easy path, but I was certain it wasn't God's path for us.

When it came time to move, we had just $450 in our bank account. I had two cavities filled the day we left. That morning, the car wouldn't start, and it died again while on the way home from the dentist. We had it towed—it was hit by *another* car on the way to the shop. Finally, late that afternoon, we loaded up and headed out in our rental truck and dented car.

About two and a half hours out of town, the engine on the truck blew up. We had to transfer all our belongings to a new truck. We finally found a hotel and collapsed on the bed, exhausted. Terri looked at me and said, "Just say it again: You are SURE we are supposed to move to Kansas City?"

The transition was hard. We weren't prepared for a harsh Missouri winter in our lightweight clothing. Terri got a job downtown, but had to ride the bus to work, which cut into our already meager budget. Things were so tight financially that if some visiting friends hadn't brought the turkey, we would've eaten Spam for our Thanksgiving meal at Midwestern.

But it wasn't all bad. I met many people in Kansas City who made a great impact on my life. I met Charlie Draper, who became my first pastor when I left seminary. Charlie taught me how to study the Word. I also met Ron Dunn and heard the great missionary, Bertha Smith, during those days. We were often hungry and cold, but we wouldn't trade our time there for anything.

Following the will of God doesn't make us exempt from trouble. The book of James tells us not to be surprised when we face trials because they are an inevitable part of life. If you are alive, you will face trials. The question comes in your response: Are you going to seek the will of God or try to convince God that your will and way are best?

By faith in God's powerful promise, I know that "all things work together for the good of those who love God" (Romans 8:28), even when I can't see how. I can trust God to show me His will. Through faith and wisdom, I see the heart of God and trust in His

> **If you are alive, you will face trials.**

purpose and plan for my life. And you can too. Even when things go wrong, know that God has not abandoned His purpose.

God's Guidance Is Sure

If you are seeking God's will, at some point someone is bound to tell you that you made the wrong decision. There are people who second-guessed the prophets for speaking out so much. They questioned Jesus when He said it wasn't time to go to Jerusalem. And they questioned Him when He said it *was* time to go to Jerusalem.

I'm sure someone told Martin Luther to keep his ninety-five theses to himself when he single-handedly sparked the Protestant Reformation. They told William Carey not to go to the mission field before he reached countless people by translating the Bible into their languages and became known as the "father of modern missions." I imagine they told D. L. Moody that an uneducated man can't start a college.

"They" are often wrong.

It would be out of character for God to leave us without directions. The One who sets the stars on their course, who made the universe, who put all things in order—would He then create man and leave us to guess about what He wants us to do?

In considering God's willingness to guide us, I believe there are several things we can know for sure:

- God loves us unconditionally; we can trust a God like that.
- God wants to speak to us and guide us through His Word.
- God's Spirit will confirm His Word and guide us into all truth.
- God has a purpose for our lives.

If God cared enough to die for us, He cares enough to guide us. Think about it:

- God led Noah to build the ark.
- God led Abraham to leave his comfort zone and set out for a new land.
- God led Joseph even when it didn't seem like God was anywhere to be found. Joseph said to his brothers, "You meant it for evil, but God used it for good."
- God led His people out of Egypt and into the Promised Land.
- God led Samuel to anoint as king a shepherd boy named David.
- God led Paul to carry the gospel to the Gentiles.

It's not that we don't want to know the will of God, but sometimes we are afraid of what God might want us to do. We may even think that God's will means doing something we don't want to do. Somehow we have bought the lie that following God might not work out for our good. Much of what Christians really believe about the will of God has no biblical basis.

Another error we can make is believing that a bad decision in our past will keep us from finding God's will today. Jeremiah reminds us that when God finds a flawed and marred vessel, He doesn't throw it away; He remakes it (Jeremiah 18:4). Never put a limit on what God will do if you'll get back in step with Him.

I've met people who assume that a closed door today is a closed door forever. But God's delay is not always His denial. It may be a matter of timing.

Yielding to the will of God is nothing less than giving God rule of your life. It's not about being willing to do a particular thing; it's being willing to do anything God asks of you.

Once you know the will of God, obedience is not optional. Don't waste your time trying to negotiate or bargain with God. Those are Satan's tactics. If you take that path, you may avoid obeying God for a time, but ultimately your plans will not succeed. John Calvin said, "God cannot approve of anything that is not supported by His Word."

God's Word Is Our Compass

In 2008, Sir Edmund Hillary died at age eighty-eight. Hillary was the first to scale the 29,035-foot summit of Mount Everest, the world's tallest peak. In the history of exploits and exploration, it's one of the greatest. His climb ranks with the first trek to the South Pole by Roald Amundsen in 1911 and the first solo nonstop trans-Atlantic flight by Charles Lindbergh in 1927.

All three men had something in common: they used a compass to direct their course. Boy Scouts and famous explorers alike use this simple tool to keep their bearings. The compass for fireproofing our decisions is the Word of God. It is the basis for guidance and direction.

God's will as it's given to us in God's Word is His best for us. Satan wants to deceive us into thinking it's not. The Enemy and our flesh will want us to rely on our feelings.

Caleb struggles with this in *Fireproof.*

EXT. DRIVEWAY
CALEB sits in his truck talking on his mobile phone.
Phone ringing.

> **JOHN**
> Hello?

> **CALEB**
> It's not working, Dad.

JOHN
What's not working?

CALEB
This whole love dare thing. It's not working!

JOHN
Tell me what's going on.

CALEB
I have been doing everything that it says to do, and she has completely rejected all of it.

JOHN
Caleb, this process takes forty days, not four.

CALEB
What is the point of going down a dead-end road when you know it's not going anywhere?

JOHN
You don't know that yet. Caleb, you're not a quitter. And something tells me you're doing just enough to get by. Am I right?

CALEB
(sighs) I *feel* nothing.

JOHN
I understand, son. This is not based on feelings. It's a decision. You can't give up yet. Keep taking a day at a time.

CALEB
Yes sir.

Fortunately for Caleb, he has a wise father who has learned that decisions should not be based solely on feelings. God never does His deepest work in the shallowest part of our being. Feelings can deceive us. We may think we know what is best based on our feelings, but often we are wrong.

The best way to fireproof your life is to bathe your decision-making in the Word of God. He never guides you to make a decision inconsistent with His Word.

As we seek God's will in our decisions, the Lord makes many areas of His purpose clear. It is a mistake to think that God hides His will from us and that somehow we are left to figure it out on our own. In many cases, fireproof decision-making is as simple as obeying the clear instructions of Scripture. You just have to look for it. And if those instructions go against your feelings, then you can be sure that your feelings are the ones misguiding you.

The Bible tells us that it is God's will for us to be:

- Saved,
- Spirit-filled,
- Sanctified,
- Submissive to authority, and
- Sexually pure (among other things).

Let's be honest, the parts of the Bible that we have the most trouble with are not the parts we don't understand, but the parts we *do* understand.

These are nonnegotiable no-brainers:

- Obey your parents. (Ephesians 6:1)

- Give of your resources. (2 Corinthians 8–9)
- Live a life of praise. (1 Thessalonians 5:16)
- Pray. (1 Thessalonians 5:17)
- Gather with other believers in church. (Hebrews 10:25)

You don't have to pray to know what God wants in these areas. They are clearly stated as the desire of God in Scripture.

A Compass for Personal Direction

There are personal issues in our lives that the Bible does not address. There is nothing specific in God's Word, for example, about what video games you should play, what music you should listen to, the appropriate age for dating, or what career path you should choose. How do we make decisions that glorify God in these areas and others?

Here are some basic questions to ask yourself to make sure your life aligns with Scripture:

- Will this lead to a deeper love for Christ and greater maturity?
- Does this have the power to control me?
- What are my motives behind this choice?
- Will this violate the lordship of Christ in my life?
- Will this be a positive witness to the lost or other believers?

Although God's Word does not give us specifics about many other day-to-day choices and decisions, it assures us that the Lord will lead us in our personal lives:

- "I will instruct you and show you the way to go; with My eye on you, I will give counsel." (Psalm 32:8)
- "Trust in the LORD with all your heart, and do not rely on your own understanding; think about Him in all your ways, and He will guide you on the right paths." (Proverbs 3:5–6)
- "Whenever you turn to the right or to the left, your ears will hear this command behind you: 'This is the way. Walk in it.'" (Isaiah 30:21)
- "This is what the LORD, your Redeemer, the Holy One of Israel says: I am Yahweh your God, who teaches you for your benefit, who leads you in the way you should go." (Isaiah 48:17)

George Müller wrote, "I never remember in all my Christian life that I ever sincerely and patiently sought to know the will of God by the teaching of the Spirit, through the Word, without being directed clearly and rightly." Over time he developed a tested method for seeking God's will.

> I seek as the beginning to get my heart into such a state that it has no will of its own in regard to a given matter. . . . Nine-tenths of the difficulties are overcome when our hearts are ready to do the Lord's will, whatever it may be. . . . Having done this, I do not leave the result to feeling or simple

impression. If so, I make myself liable to great delusions.

I seek the will of the Spirit of God through, or in connection with, the Word of God. . . . Next I take into account providential circumstances. These often plainly indicate God's will in connection with His Word and Spirit.

I ask God in prayer to reveal His will to me aright.

Thus, through prayer to God, the study of the Word, and reflection, I come to a deliberate judgment. . . . In trivial matters, and in transactions involving most important issues, I have found this method always effective.[1]

Making fireproof decisions begins and ends with a desire to do the will of God. Safe decision-making will never happen if we try to convince our Father to see things our way.

Ron Dunn preached the best message on finding God's will that I've ever heard. It was based on Romans 12:1–2. He ended that message with three guidelines.

> **Making fireproof decisions begins and ends with a desire to do the will of God.**

The first is desire. "Take delight in the LORD, and He will give you your heart's desires" (Psalm 37:4). If we are committed to delighting ourselves in the Lord, we can assume that our delight, His desires, and our desires will line up.

The second is opportunity. Desire alone is not enough. Some of our own desires can be selfish, but desires that come from God are always accompanied by an open door. Where He guides, He provides. God's leading begins with desire and is confirmed by opportunity.

The final guideline is humility, leaning on God for continued clarity. We learn this one from Balaam's donkey. Balaam tried to justify his actions (Numbers 22). He talked himself into believing something was right that wasn't. Ron explained that even when we "feel right" and "have a peace," we can misread our own heart. When in doubt, don't.

There are no distinctions between big and little issues, big and little obedience, in the will of God. From our perspective, we might think a certain decision is no big deal, but the magnitude of that decision may affect us years down the road.

All of us have made decisions we regret. Maybe you've made a poor choice in your life and still bear the scars today. The choices you make now affect you for the rest of your life. Even the most godly people make wrong choices. But some people think the will of God is like Humpty Dumpty—a wrong choice means they can never put their lives back together again.

Nothing could be further from the truth!

Maybe you've blown it in the past. Maybe you've been burned. You can't change the past, but you can do something to safeguard yourself in the days ahead.

John Wesley—revivalist and founder of Methodism—struggled to know the will of God in his personal life, yet was greatly used to bring many to Christ.

Fearing marriage would distract him from ministry, Wesley still found himself drawn, at the age of thirty-two, to a young lady he met while serving in Georgia. After drawing an "answer" from a hat, he concluded he was to "think of it no more." Later in life he fell in love with another woman but was influenced to avoid matrimony in this case, as well.

Finally, in his late forties, Wesley married a wealthy widow named Mary Vazeille. It was a very unhappy marriage, and she eventually left him. Wesley wrote in his journal, "I have not left her; I would not send her away; I will not recall her."[2]

Obviously, God used Wesley even though he had a terrible and tragic marriage. Finding the will of God is not about waving a magic wand or seeing what the majority of your friends think. How do you know the will of God? How can you fireproof the decisions of your life? We won't always make perfect decisions, but we can have a biblical approach to decision-making.

If we get right down to it and can't discern what the good, acceptable, and perfect will of God is for our lives, the following questions will likely pinpoint the trouble:

- Do you believe that God's will can be known definitely and accurately? (Psalm 32:8; Isaiah 30:21)
- Are you willing to seek God's will and do it, or would you just like to know it as an option? (John 7:17)
- Have you made a permanent decision of commitment to be yielded to God for the rest of your life? (Romans 12:1–2)
- Is there any known unconfessed sin in your life? If so, stop here and confess it and leave it behind you. (Psalm 66:18; Proverbs 28:13; 1 John 1:9)
- Are you obeying the known will of God for your life on a daily basis? If not, start today and demonstrate your obedience before going on. (Psalm 119:59–60)
- Are you in neutral? Are you willing to go either way on this issue? Ask God that His desires will be your desires. (Philippians 2:13)
- Are you praying specifically and definitely about it in faith? Make a list of your specific thoughts and pray about them by faith. (Mark 10:51; James 1:5–7)
- Are you spending time with God daily in prayer and Bible study? If not, begin today. (Psalm 5:3)
- Have you sought the counsel of spiritually mature people? (Proverbs 11:14; 12:15; 15:22; 19:20; 20:18; 24:6)
- Are you willing to wait in faith for God to line up His Word, your peace, and the circumstances? (Hebrews 10:36)

- Do you have an inner conviction or peace about your course of action? (Romans 14:23)
- Will it bring glory to God? (1 Corinthians 10:31; Colossians 3:17)

Testing Our Decisions

In life we're going to have tests, fire drills if you will, that give us opportunities to make God-honoring decisions. When we study the life of Abraham, we realize that God used every test in the book to grow Abraham in his faith.

In Genesis 22:1–10, God put Abraham to the ultimate test. The command of God to offer up his son Isaac as a sacrifice is as real as it gets. It's easy to say we want to honor God in our decision-making, but the reality of our words is revealed when the test hits close to home.

Where Satan may tempt us into doing evil, God tests us to bring out our best. Abraham's test involved the heir to the promise, the joy of his life. Here we see a man who teaches that we can love God and make right decisions even when His leading appears to be illogical or costly. I heard Vance Havner say, "When we go through God's testing properly, all we lose are the shackles that tied us up earlier."

Have you considered that God's tests are evidence that He trusts us—or more accurately, He trusts Himself to keep us? His intention is not that our faith will fail, but develop. We should remember that God always prepares us for the test. Genesis 22:1 says, "After these things God tested Abraham and said to him, 'Abraham!' 'Here I am,' he answered." What things? All the other tests. God didn't want Isaac's life; He wanted Abraham's heart.

Look at Abraham's decision-making process. When God told him to sacrifice his son, he responded immediately. He didn't wait, didn't argue, didn't negotiate. Abraham obeyed. Someone has said, "True spirituality is often measured by the length of response time to God's commands." This is where many believers get hung up and ultimately get derailed. But Abraham obeyed because he believed God. He knew that God would provide.

Typically we go through tests in the area of our possessions (how we use them), our plans (how we yield them), and people (how we treat them). It is doubtful that God can use us in a significant way until we have passed these tests. It's meaningless to pray, "God, use me," if we aren't willing for God to make us usable.

When we think about Abraham, we can observe a powerful truth: Whatever we cling to is usually what God asks for.

Ron Dunn preached a classic message on this passage in which he said, "Isaac was God's idea; now He's going to take him away. In verse two, God is twisting the knife. 'Thy son, thy only son, Isaac, whom you love . . .' Isaac was the culmination of God's work and plan. Isaac was spared. God never intended for Isaac to die. Somebody died on that mountain; it was Abraham. He had to die to Isaac. God knew until He had Isaac, He didn't have all of Abraham. Until Isaac was on the altar, God was not on the throne."

We say we want to make godly decisions, but all too often, in reality we don't want to give up the thing that is our pride and joy. We must become like Abraham, voluntarily and deliberately choosing the will of God.

A sixteenth-century believer wrote, "After having given myself wholly to God . . . I renounced, for the love of Him, everything that was not He; and I began to live as if there were none but He and I in the world."[3] It's this process, this continual giving of ourselves completely to God, that will make our decisions more aligned with His. As we begin to know God through His Word and by spending time with Him, we begin to want the things that He wants. Our natural ability to make God-centered decisions grows stronger until one day, that decision-making ability becomes fireproof.

Fire Drill!

1. Was there a time in your life when you clearly felt God leading you? What happened?

2. Can you think of a time when you made a decision based on your feelings and regretted it? What can you learn from that experience?

3. Pages 95–96 list some of God's clear instructions in the Bible. Which of these do you have the most trouble following?

4. How can you use God's Word as a compass?

5. Take a moment to review what you learned in this chapter and create your own process for decision-making. Write this process down and keep it where you can refer to it when you have a decision to make.

CHAPTER 7

Fireproof Relationships

*Catch the foxes for us—the little foxes that ruin the
vineyards—for our vineyards are in bloom.*

—SONG OF SONGS 2:15

Relationships are hard work, but people don't always work
hard at them. As a teenager, you've no doubt seen your
share of makeups and breakups around you. Although less
frequently (I hope), you've also seen friendships grow apart,
relationships with parents become strained, and even difficult relationships with teachers, coaches, and other leaders.

You've probably also noticed in the families around
you that divorce has become the norm rather than the
exception—both within the church and without. Although

marriage and the risk of divorce may not even be a blip on your radar right now, other relationships most definitely are. And by learning *right now* how to build and maintain healthy relationships, you can later apply those lessons to all of the relationships in your future—including your marriage.

In the movie *Fireproof,* Caleb and Catherine Holt have been married for seven years. Although once in love, they have grown apart and are headed for divorce. Tension fills every conversation. Self-centeredness leads to countless arguments, which lead to finger-pointing and exaggeration.

Any of that sound familiar? Have conversations between you and your parents grown tense? When you have a fight with friends, who takes the blame? When you fight with your brother or sister, do you hear a lot of, "I always . . . !" and "You never . . . !"? All of these ineffective behaviors in relationships can carry through to your adult relationships. They can truly ruin the rest of your life if you don't learn more effective methods for expressing your frustrations and how to handle people with a generous helping of grace.

The problem in many relationships is at the very foundation. As with Caleb and Catherine, they lack something or someone to hold them together and restore their lost love—that someone is Jesus Christ. But when Caleb finds Christ and begins to love Catherine the way Christ loves the church, the tables begin to turn.

At one point in the movie, Caleb has come to Christ, but Catherine is still skeptical. She has seen a change, but she's not sure why. She doubts Caleb's motives. One day while Catherine is sick in bed, Caleb brings her medicine and begins to open his heart to her.

INT. MASTER BEDROOM
CATHERINE sits up in the bed; CALEB sitting at her bedside.

> **CALEB**
> Here. (hands CATHERINE medicine)
> You think you can take this?

> **CATHERINE**
> (swallows medicine) Why are you doing this?

> **CALEB**
> I have learned, you never leave
> your partner, especially in a fire.

As a culture, we seem to have lost our stamina in relationships. When things get rough, we move on to the next friend. When we have a hard time in a class, it's the teacher's fault. If our church insults us, we find a new church family. But Caleb disrupts what society has accepted as normal when he decides to fight for his family.

> **CATHERINE**
> Caleb, I don't know how to process this.
> This is not normal for you.

> **CALEB**
> Welcome to the new normal.

As we fireproof our relationships, might I suggest that we throw out society's idea of normal and begin to pursue relationships the way God intended them?

You may not be fighting to save your marriage—not today, anyway. But as Caleb fights for his, he has some realizations that could help us all as we develop and maintain our own relationships.

CALEB

I need you to know something, Catherine. I'm sorry . . . I have been so selfish. For the last seven years, I've trampled on you with my words and actions. I've loved other things when I should have loved you. In the last few weeks, God has given me a love for you that I've never had before. I've asked Him to forgive me and have been hoping . . . praying that you would somehow be able to forgive me too.

On the surface, it sounds like a sweet, sincere apology from a guy trying to win back the girl. But if you'll look closely, you'll see that this one brief cinematic moment contains five essential elements of a successful relationship—whether that is with your friends, your family, or eventually, your lifelong spouse.

- Communication
- Care and concern
- Commitment
- Confession
- Christ-like love

Communication. Every living thing—plants, animals, people—needs nourishment to survive. When you communicate, you are nourishing your relationships. Communication has little to do with being extroverted and everything to do with helping your relationships to grow emotionally, verbally, and spiritually.

Even when it's difficult to say what you're feeling, you need to communicate to the other person how you feel if that relationship is ever going to stand the test of fire. This one can be awkward at first, especially if you're out of practice with articulating your thoughts and feelings. (Girls seem to be better at this; guys, we need to practice.)

Caleb starts with, "I need you to know something." Easy enough, right? Although it can be embarrassing or risky, don't let a little temporary awkwardness get in the way of a lifelong relationship. Usually that "awkwardness" is just a point of discomfort that you have to get past in order to grow. Real relationships can't subsist entirely on talk about the weather, gossip, or last night's football game. They have to be rooted in real things, progressive things—hopes and dreams and fears—and conquering those things through continued support of one another.

So whatever it is you need the other person to know, *tell them.* Write a letter, send a text, or even better, say it in person, over a milkshake or a cup of coffee. The rewards of a strong, long-lasting relationship far outweigh the temporary discomfort of getting your feelings out in the open. And once you overcome the initial awkwardness, be sure to regularly nourish your relationships with open-flowing communication.

Care and concern. Caleb admits to being selfish, to caring only about himself and his own wants and needs. But as he's learned, there are two people in a relationship. And the other person's wants and needs matter too.

Do you gobble up the last brownie without a second thought? Do you always make your little brother play *your* favorite game? Do you spend an hour in the bathroom with no regard for whoever else may need to get ready? When you make a habit of always getting your way, doing everything the way you want, you're setting yourself up for a lonely life. Not only do you gradually isolate yourself from people who want to spend time with you, but you also close yourself off to what you can learn from doing things *other* ways, the way someone else wants to do them.

Caleb also admits to being careless with his words and actions. So many of us are. We snap back at others, spewing out the first thing that comes to mind. Or we instinctually react with no thought of the other person's feelings.

Proverbs has a lot to say about the power of the "tongue":

- "The tongue of the righteous is pure silver; the heart of the wicked is of little value." (Proverbs 10:20)
- "The mouth of the righteous produces wisdom, but a perverse tongue will be cut out." (Proverbs 10:31)
- "There is one who speaks rashly, like a piercing sword; but the tongue of the wise brings healing." (Proverbs 12:18)

- "Truthful lips endure forever, but a lying tongue, only a moment." (Proverbs 12:19)
- "The tongue of the wise makes knowledge attractive, but the mouth of fools blurts out foolishness." (Proverbs 15:2)
- "The tongue that heals is a tree of life, but a devious tongue breaks the spirit." (Proverbs 15:4)
- "Life and death are in the power of the tongue, and those who love it will eat its fruit." (Proverbs 18:21)

Did you notice that most of these verses give you two options? The power of the tongue can be used for good or evil, to heal or hurt, to bring life or death in our relationships and in our lives in general. Choose to use your power for good, to heal, to bring life.

As powerful as the tongue can be, our actions are even more so. Actions most certainly speak louder than even the loudest words. If you love someone, show them. If you're sorry, say it in your actions. If you think their feelings are important, then by all means, let them see that in the way you act when they're around.

The way we treat others has effects that reach far beyond the confines of our relationships. The way we treat others shows new believers and nonbelievers how they will be treated by Christians. The way we treat others sets an example of Christ for the entire world to see. Jesus Himself told us, "By this all people will know that you are My disciples, if you have love for one another" (John 13:35). Handle

God's people with care, not only for the sake of your own relationships, but for the sake of the Kingdom.

Commitment. Caleb admits to loving other things, when he should have been loving his wife. For one, he's poured all of his extra money into saving for a boat for himself. He's also struggled with pornography. Whether or not you share these particular struggles, there are a vast variety of other ways we can lack commitment in our attitudes and actions toward others.

Do you text your way through family dinners? Stare at the cute guy across campus when your friend is confiding in you? Do you roll your eyes to your friends when talking to your dad on the phone?

What messages do you send through your interactions with others?

In the Song of Songs, we read, "Catch the foxes for us—the little foxes that ruin the vineyards—for our vineyards are in bloom" (2:15). Foxes get into vineyards to feed on the grapes, and the keepers must prop up the branches so the foxes can't reach them. Warren Wiersbe says that the "little foxes" represent those little things that quietly destroy relationships. Greed, envy, disrespect, discourteousness—these and others are all small little foxes that can nibble away at the bonds of a relationship. Prop up the branches—protect your relationships from the things of this world.

Be committed to being present and being respectful during your time with your parents, your family, and your friends. Don't let insignificant things—like electronics or some random guy or trying to look cool—get in the way of true relationships. Be sure that both your actions and your words show your commitment to the people you love.

Confession. Caleb begins his words with an apology; he ends by asking for forgiveness. And everything in the middle is his confession to his wife. We are all going to royally mess things up on occasion, and there's really only one way to move past that.

James 5:16 tells us how: "Therefore, confess your sins to one another and pray for one another, so that you may be healed." You've got to confess what you did wrong, say it out loud, ask for forgiveness. Any relationship worth keeping will honor this request, respect you for your honesty, and grow even stronger as a result.

Confession will take awkwardness to a whole new level, but rip off the bandage. Just say it. You have to confess so that you may be healed.

Christ-like love. Caleb tells Catherine, "God has given me a love for you that I've never had before." When we honor God in our relationships, He will bless them. He will pour His mercy and grace over them and allow them to grow with a Christ-like love.

But be sure to note, here, that a Christ-like love isn't just some teen magazine tip for a good relationship. This is a command from Jesus Himself: "I give you a new command: Love one another. Just as I have loved you, you must also love one another" (John 13:34).

So how did Jesus love us? He gave us wisdom, healing, hope, forgiveness, compassion, strength, and faith. Paul describes love in 1 Corinthians 13:4–8:

> Love is patient, love is kind. Love does not envy, is not boastful, is not conceited, does not act improperly, is not selfish, is not provoked, and does not keep a record of wrongs. Love finds no joy in unrighteousness but rejoices in the truth. It bears all things, believes all things, hopes all things, endures all things. Love never ends.

With a Christ-like love in place, kindness is a no-brainer. Compassion is ever-present. Honesty is a given. Humility bows in respect. In a Christ-like relationship, confessions are met with grace and followed by forgiveness. A Christ-like love is not easy, but it is our goal. It is what we all must strive for in all of our relationships.

YOU Are the Culture Changers

When is the last time you saw Christ-like love reflected in primetime television? I'd say it's been a while! But it's really not the television's fault. The sitcoms and reality shows that stay on the air reflect our culture, what our culture wants to see, and what our culture will allow.

It's up to you to change that. And I'm not just talking about television. Relationships in general are a mess—it's true. But cleaning them up starts with you.

Let's show the world how Christ loves. Let's show the world that relationships aren't disposable, that families are the foundations of our lives. Let's shush the critics and let compassion reign. Let's give a little grace, sprinkle a little forgiveness, and see what grows.

My guess?

A Christ-like love that stands tall, that holds close, that grows even stronger after the fire.

Fire Drill!

1. When's the last time Mom got the last brownie? Imagine her happiness if you were to take it to her on a plate, bestowing upon Mom the last-brownie honors. Or better yet, make a batch yourself for the whole family to enjoy!

2. Take a look at a concordance or do an electronic search of the Bible to find other references to the "tongue." How can you apply these verses to your relationships?

3. Think about your closest relationships. Is there anything that you need to confess so that you can receive healing? Find a way to seek forgiveness today.

4. Describe a Christ-like love. If you need help, look through the Gospels to see the way that Christ loved people.

5. What are some ways that you and your friends can spread a Christ-like love around your community, starting today?

CHAPTER 8

Fireproof Money

"For where your treasure is,
there your heart will be also."

—MATTHEW 6:21

A critical area in which Satan constantly seeks a foothold in our lives is finances. A Christian who will not obey God in the area of money finds it harder to resist sin in other areas of life and is a poor witness for Christ. The writer of Proverbs said, "Honor the LORD with your possessions and with the first produce of your entire harvest; then your barns will be completely filled, and your vats will overflow with new wine" (3:9–10). Giving back to God is the first principle of godly financial planning.

Several years ago, I preached a series called "Putting Your Financial House in Order." During that series, I shared a story I heard from John Maxwell. A father took his young son to a fast-food restaurant for lunch. When asked what he wanted to eat, the little boy said, "I want French fries." The father placed the order and even super-sized the meal. They found a table, said the blessing, and started eating. The dad finished his meal first, then reached for one of his son's fries. The boy put his arms over the fries and said defiantly, "These are MY fries!"

The boy obviously forgot a few things. First, he forgot that his father was the source of the fries: his dad took him to the restaurant, paid for the meal, and even carried the tray. He also forgot that his father didn't need his son's French fries; he could have easily bought his own. Finally, the son forgot that his dad had chosen to super-size the order to begin with. He did it because he wanted to give generously to his son.

God Is a Giver

Since the dawning of creation, God has modeled giving for us:

- He gave Adam and Eve a beautiful garden to live in.
- He gave the Israelites a pillar of cloud for protection, a pillar of fire for guidance, and manna from heaven to feed them.
- He gave the Israelites the Promised Land.

- He gave a kingship to David, a shepherd boy.
- He gave us His Son to die in our place.
- He gave us the Holy Spirit to guide us.

Our God is a giving God. His greatest expression of giving is not found in possessions but in the person of Jesus Christ. Christ continues to give to us through His love, mercy, forgiveness, grace, peace, and power. We are debtors to God, and we owe Him everything.

If we want to follow the example of our heavenly Father, giving is not an option. Yet one area where believers kick and scream the most is stewardship. If we don't get that right, though, we'll never live abundant lives.

One scene in *Fireproof* is a great example of this type of kicking-and-screaming stewardship. In this case, however, Caleb has been asked to give something nice to his wife. But his attitude about giving says it all.

```
INT. FIRE HALL, OFFICE
CALEB is talking on the telephone.
```

CALEB

Yeah, uh, I need to order some flowers
or something for my wife.
(listens)
No, no, it doesn't matter.
(listens)
Sure. How much does that cost?
(listens)
Forty-five?! Do you have something cheaper?
(listens)

Yeah, yeah, that's more like it.
Let's go with the twenty-five.
(listens)
How 'bout, um, how 'bout a box of chocolates
or something? How much is that?
(listens)
Agh, you're killing me!
(listens, nods)
That's better. Okay, how about a little,
a little stuffed bear?
(listens)
All right, forget the bear. Okay, how
long's it gonna take you to throw
something like that together?

Needless to say, when Catherine got home, she dismissed the sad bouquet with as much thought as Caleb had put into it.

You may think you have little to give right now. You may only have an allowance, a minimum-wage-paying part-time job, or no income at all. That's okay. God only wants you to give from what you have. And money is not the only way to give.

My parents were not rich people. My dad was a pharmacist. He owned his own store for a number of years until he had to close the doors. It so happened that the year he did, I was headed to a private college to begin studying for the ministry. I learned something about the faithfulness of God from my dad during that time.

My dad had taught me never to go into debt. He also taught me to tithe. He gave 25 to 30 percent of his income to the church. He didn't always agree with the preacher, but he knew that he was giving his gift to the Lord. Another principle my dad taught me was sacrifice. He knew that God had called me into the ministry, and he sacrificed greatly so that I could go to college. I am indebted to my dad for teaching me these truths early in life.

Today, Terri and I also give more than a tithe. We not only tithe to our church, but we also give sacrificially to our building program and other ministries. We give "over and above" for the joy of giving. Every Sunday, even after paying our tithes and offerings, we put something more in the plate in both services. We just don't want to come to church empty-handed. I'm learning the lesson that all I have is a sacred trust. None of it is mine; it *all* belongs to Him.

Giving Ourselves

Now, before you skip over this part, let me beg you to take these truths to heart. This issue is crucial to the Christian life. Stewardship is lordship. This principle is captured in the story of a little boy who saw the offering plate going by. He didn't have any money, so he tore off a part of the bulletin and scribbled on it, "I give myself."

This is exactly what the Macedonian believers did. Paul wrote to the Corinthians and told them about the Macedonian church:

> We want you to know, brothers, about the grace
> of God granted to the churches of Macedonia:

During a severe testing by affliction, their abundance of joy and their deep poverty overflowed into the wealth of their generosity. I testify that, on their own, according to their ability and beyond their ability, they begged us insistently for the privilege of sharing in the ministry to the saints, and not just as we had hoped. Instead, they gave themselves especially to the Lord, then to us by God's will. (2 Corinthians 8:1–5)

Can you imagine being that committed to the work of God?

An angel in Milton's classic *Paradise Lost* could, by the touch of a certain spear, reveal the true character of a person. Similarly, the way we think about and use money gives good insight into who we really are. We may not give money away, but money will give us away.

If we don't learn to have God's perspective on our finances, we will make greed our god, and all that we earn or own will one day be gone. We must learn to lay up treasure in heaven, where taxes and gas prices can't get to it. Otherwise, our only legacy will be a big yard sale when we're gone.

I did a funeral years ago for a man whose family spent lavishly for his funeral. They bought the most expensive mahogany casket and copper vault—investing tens of thousands of dollars to be covered with dirt. As far as I could tell, the man had never invested in eternal things.

I've watched others (even people in the church) buy houses and lands while never laying up treasures in heaven. It is possible to come to church and sing songs about God, but refuse Him entry into our wallets.

You Can't Out-Give God

What we do with our money represents who we are— our time, toil, and talent. Someone once said, "Money is concentrated personality, or personality in coin. Our picture may not be on any bill, but our person is certainly in it." If our attitude and actions do not follow the example of the Macedonians, we'll have nothing to show for our lives when we get to heaven.

In his book *As You Sow*, Bill Bright wrote the following:

> Many years ago, Dr. Oswald Smith, the famous Canadian evangelist and missionary statesman, spoke on stewardship to his congregation. "You can't beat God at giving," he said. "If you will deal honorably with God in money matters, obeying the command to bring all the tithes into the storehouse, God will prosper you spiritually and materially."[1]

I have found this to be true. Whenever I've taken a church position, I've never asked about the salary before agreeing to come. I've trusted God with my pay, and He has always been faithful. Some churches have been generous, others have not, but God has always provided. If we first give ourselves—whatever that may mean for you, wherever you are financially—God knows how to provide for those who take their stewardship seriously.

Our world system is backwards. We've become convinced that winning the lottery or gambling will make us rich, successful, and happy. Read the stories of those who have bought into this myth. People lie to them, steal from them, and often they are unhappy in the long run. Many end up bankrupt. Why? They don't understand God's plan of economy. We think *getting* is the answer to all our problems, but in God's economy, *giving* is the answer. Through our giving, we understand that Christ supplies all our needs according to His riches in glory in Christ Jesus.

> **We think *getting* is the answer to all our problems, but in God's economy, *giving* is the answer.**

In the gospel of Matthew, Jesus gave us a clear warning and an eternal principle:

"Don't collect for yourselves treasures on earth, where moth and rust destroy and where thieves break in and steal. But collect for yourselves treasures in heaven, where neither moth nor rust destroys, and where thieves don't break in and steal. For where your treasure is, there your heart will be also." (6:19–21)

Greed Is Not Gain

Finances are the root of some of the biggest problems in the home. Looking at finances from an unbiblical perspective results in bondage and debt that will cost more than we can imagine. Because of the greed of my generation, we are now raising a materialistic "I want it now" generation. And who are we as parents to criticize? We're the ones who created the mindset that if you want it, you can have it *now*.

Every Sunday there are those who leave the church as soon as the preacher says, "Amen." Many fail to worship and honor God with their lips and their gifts. In reality, though, they sacrifice their own lives on things that are frivolous and temporary.

Because of this greed, we are also neglecting an investment in missions. Many believers have no vision for missions and ministry because they are walking around in a fog of selfishness. Remember Achan in Joshua 7? He stole what belonged to the Lord, and it cost him and his entire family their lives. He said, "I saw," "I coveted," and "I took." That's a danger in our media-driven society. We see stuff, we want it, and we take it, even if it means disobeying God in the process.

"For the love of money is a root of all kinds of evil, and by craving it, some have wandered away from the faith and pierced themselves with many pains" (1 Timothy 6:10). Warren Wiersbe says Paul shared four facts with Timothy to warn us about the dangers of wanting what we do not have:

1. Wealth does not bring contentment (1 Timothy 6:6). The word *contentment* means an inner sufficiency that keeps us at peace in spite of outward circumstances. True contentment comes from godliness in the heart, not wealth in the hand.
2. Wealth is not lasting (v. 7). Whatever wealth we earn goes to the government, our heirs, and maybe charity and the church. We all know the answer to the question, "How much did he leave [when he died]?" Everything!
3. Our basic needs are easily met (v. 8). Food, clothing, and shelter are basic needs. If we lose them, we lose the ability to secure other things. Henry David Thoreau, the naturalist of the 1800s, reminded us that a man is wealthy in proportion to the number of things he can afford to do without.
4. The desire for wealth leads to sin (vv. 9–10). "They that will be rich," is the accurate translation. It describes a person who must have more and more material things in order to be happy and feel successful. But riches are a trap, and they lead to bondage, not freedom. Instead of giving satisfaction, riches create additional desires, and these must be satisfied.[2]

In my early days at Sherwood, Jonathan Beasley was our youth minister. He had an ingenious way of controlling his spending. To keep himself from making an impulsive purchase, he kept his credit card frozen in ice in his freezer. If he went shopping and found something he thought he "had to have," he would go home and let the card thaw out. If he still "needed" it after going home and thinking about it, he could go back for it. Some of us need to freeze our spending so we can free our giving.

Beyond the Tithe

If the Macedonians could give out of their poverty, why don't we give out of our prosperity? You may not feel very prosperous, but if you have any spending money whatsoever, you have something to tithe from. Some tithe for years but never give a penny more than ten percent. Those people miss out on the joy of giving. They obey the law, but perhaps they haven't bought into grace. Giving as unto the Lord in light of grace moves us beyond percentages. It makes us want to give our life, our love, our all.

So learn this lesson now: God meets our needs when we learn to be generous. If we give both when we can afford it *and* when we can't, God makes ends meet. I don't know how He does it, but I know that He does.

I once heard a preacher talk on giving, and it changed everything I knew about stewardship. He said, "Since the garden of Eden, God has set aside something for Himself as a reminder to man that everything is the Lord's." Then he nailed me with a truth I can't get over: "God always reserves something for Himself in the physical realm, where man obtains his living, to remind man that God is the owner of everything. God reserved for Himself a tree, a day, a city, the tithe, a year when the land was to stand idle." The facts here are clear. What God sets aside as holy, as His, is a reminder that we are stewards, not owners. And when we hoard what belongs to God, it opens the door for moths and rust to destroy all we have.

It has taken me a lifetime to learn these principles. So take it from me, start applying these truths to your life now, and just watch how God will bless your life. As you set out to build your own financial foundation, keep these guidelines in mind:

- When we have experienced grace, we should express our gratitude to God through giving.
- When Jesus is Lord, it is reflected in our giving and spending.
- When the heart is right, giving to the Lord and His work is never a burden.
- To do the work of God, we must see the need of investing in Kingdom business.
- Giving is as much a part of worship as prayer, preaching, and singing.
- Never forget the law of the harvest: You reap what you sow, you reap more than you sow, and you reap later than you sow. I can't very well ask God to help me with my finances if I'm not honoring Him in that area.
- God loves a cheerful giver. Cheer up! What you're giving is earning eternal interest.

The bottom line is this: Money will go up in flames. But treasures in heaven will last an eternity.

Fire Drill!

1. What are some gifts God has given you?

2. What are some gifts that you can give back to God?

3. Create a monthly budget with your income and expenses (however large or small). Estimate the best you can. Be sure to include a line for tithing or giving.

4. What are some ways that you can support local ministries in your community?

5. What is one step that you can take this week to build your financial foundation?

CHAPTER 9

Fireproof—
No Matter What

*Dear friends, don't be surprised when the fiery
ordeal comes among you to test you as if
something unusual were happening to you.*

—1 PETER 4:12

Everyone reading this has probably been burned at some point. Everyone has hills and valleys. Everyone goes through the fire of adversity, when there is little to offer comfort. What we need during these times of crisis is not pop psychology or peppy preaching. We need the power of

God to sustain us. We need to see our way clearly through the smoke.

You've no doubt heard people talk about the "good old days" when life seemed simpler. And maybe it was. Regardless, we don't live there anymore. Life is complex, confusing, and complicated. When I was growing up, ice cream came in three flavors: vanilla, chocolate, and strawberry. Now we have hundreds of flavors and can mix in anything we want, from gummy bears to cookies. The choices can be overwhelming!

How does our society deal with the complex crises of life? Sometimes by sticking its head in the sand. Is this how we are preparing you, the young people of today, to deal with the crises of the future? I should hope not.

Years ago on *CBS Evening News*, Charles Osgood reported on a mall that had banned baseball caps from being worn backwards because they saw it as a gang sign. "This proves," he said, "that when faced with a serious problem, we will do anything to keep from dealing with the real issue." Some wallow in problems while others deal in denial, but few take hold of a crisis and transform it into something useful.

If we don't learn from the crises of life, we're doomed to repeat our mistakes over and over. To rise above, we must learn that the fire is for our refining, so the gold can shine through in gleaming purity.

Although we know difficult times will come, we often don't prepare for them. People put off getting car or health insurance, hoping something doesn't happen—and when it does, it's often a catastrophe.

While doing a study on how leaders deal with crises, I jotted down these words about the great Indian chief, Sitting Bull:

> A product of his culture, Sitting Bull remained acutely aware of the dangers that lack of preparation could engender, and he kept himself closely attuned to all the elements of his environment that could suddenly change and plunge him into a life-threating situation. He had a plan B for every possibility.
>
> Custer too had experienced crisis during the Civil War, but . . . he had so long led the charmed life of a commander who could do no wrong that he assumed his confrontation with the Enemy would go according to plan. He thought the campaign would bring him into the White House and the Presidency. His mind was at the White House; Sitting Bull's was on the battlefield.[1]

The punch that knocks us out is not the hardest one; it's the one we don't expect.

The punch that knocks us out is not the hardest one; it's the one we don't expect.

Facing the Fires

Some people fall into the pit of failure when disaster strikes. Some shrug their shoulders and go into survival mode. The person who wants to grow in the conflict seeks to learn from it.

As a pastor, I've watched all kinds of responses to crisis:

- "Trouble happens."
- "This is just a nightmare."
- "This always happens to me."
- "It must be God's will."
- "If it's trouble, I deserve it."
- "I must have bad karma."

In reality, the issue is not the crisis itself, but how we respond to it.

Eric, a rookie firefighter, learns this lesson through experience as the firemen face different emergencies in the film *Fireproof.* In one particular scene, they've just rescued some teens from a car that had ended up on the train tracks after an accident. The car was not drivable, and there were two teen girls trapped inside. As the firemen work to extract the girls, they hear the ominous sound of a train whistle in the distance. Together, the firemen and bystanders must work to push the car off the tracks, just before the train barrels by.

Back at the fire station, the rookie firefighter begins to wonder what he's gotten himself into.

INT. FIRE HALL
ERIC and MICHAEL stand between the two fire
trucks, removing their jumpsuits and boots.

> **ERIC**
> Hey, Lieutenant?

> **MICHAEL**
> Yeah?

> **ERIC**
> This kind of thing doesn't happen
> all the time, does it?

> **MICHAEL**
> Risking our lives? Yes. Playing chicken
> with a train? First time.

> **ERIC**
> Aren't you afraid of dying?

> **MICHAEL**
> No. Because I know where *I'm* going. I just don't
> want to get there because I got hit by a train.

Michael is a firefighter. He knows that he's going to see fires on a regular basis; it's part of the job. So when he sees a fire, he doesn't freak out; he doesn't run away screaming. He is prepared. Although he knows that each situation is different, he has practiced and planned to face the danger. He goes in wearing protective gear with a truck full of tools behind him. He has years of experience, and he learns something new with each hard challenge he faces.

The same is true for us, even more so as Christians. We've signed up for this battle between good and evil, and we live in a sinful world. There are going to be big fires, catastrophic fires. But we have God, His Word, and the Holy Spirit in us, to guide us through. Each time we experience a crisis, we build our faith in preparation for the fires of the future, and we grow in wisdom that will be a light to other believers along the way. Once we accept that life is not a fairy tale, crises become less difficult to handle.

Radio broadcaster Paul Harvey once said, "In times like these, it is good to remember there have always been times like these." Some of us are so prone to being burned by the sparks of life that we whine about the slightest conflict as if no one had ever faced such difficulties. The truth is that somewhere, someone is facing a more difficult challenge than we are.

When faced with a crisis, the questions to ask are not "Why me?" or "Why this?" or "Why now?" In reality the only honest question is: "What now?" You and I aren't the first to see the sparks of adversity turn into a flaming fire all around us—and we won't be the last.

My parents, with others of their generation, lived through events I can't even begin to imagine: the stock market crash of 1929 and the Great Depression, World War II with its resulting food and gas rationing, the Korean conflict, the Cuban Missile Crisis, and much more.

As I think about all our parents lived through, the "good old days" don't seem that good. But rarely did I hear them discuss those times, much less complain about them. The problem with some of us is that we think nobody knows the trouble we've seen. We can honestly deceive ourselves into thinking our trivial disappointments are crises.

We Need Each Other

One truth I learned, that Caleb learned, while filming *Fireproof* is that a fireman never leaves his partner behind, especially in a fire. That's why it grieves me to see once-active believers who have bailed out because of a crisis. Rather than running to God, they ran away from Him and His church—the very thing they needed in their trial.

In the hardest moments of life, we need people who have been through the fire before—seasoned veterans. We may be rookies at fighting this crisis, but we can find others who have survived the battle. If we don't learn from those more experienced than we are, we forfeit the value of their example and advice.

I've been blessed with godly counsel of older men all my life. When going through a crisis, I seek their counsel, wisdom, and insight. I've learned to listen and, I hope, to apply what I've learned. Their advice has spared me much heartache. When you find yourself facing a huge dilemma or a challenging time of life, seek out older Christians who have walked down a similar road. Seek their counsel, consider their judgment, and learn from them.

And you, too, are old enough to invest yourself in younger believers. There are kids who are looking up to you right now, seeing how you handle your own difficulties; they may come to you when they have trials of their own. They need your wisdom. Seek them out; don't wait for them to find you.

One of the best things that the experience of older believers will give you is a long-term perspective. That viewpoint will help you to make decisions based on principle rather than short-term gain. My Christian parents, for example, taught me to always do the right thing—to keep your word, maintain your character, and do what's right—even if it hurts. I have found that this policy works best because the decisions you make don't come back to haunt you.

Dealing with a Crisis

Another thing that can overwhelm us in a conflict is trying to fight too many fires at once. We run here and there, throwing water on scattered fires, but we never deal with any of them completely. Often a crisis will recur because we've dealt with the symptoms, not the problem.

I once read the following: "Never try to solve all the problems all at once—make them line up for you one by one. Whether you face three problems, thirty or three hundred . . . make them stand in a single file so you can face only one at a time." This is a key to keeping your emotions balanced.

John Mason poses the question, "Is the only time you do any deep praying when you find yourself in a hole?" He goes on to say this regarding the most important aspect of crisis management: "Prayer may not change all things for you, but it sure changes you for all things. He's waiting to hear from you."[2]

If you are going through a difficult time in life, remember this: God's ear is open to your cries. Draw near to God. Get so near to Him that you can hear Him whisper in your heart. When we seek Him, we will find Him.

Good can come out of the crises of life. During the Great Chicago Fire of 1871, nearly everything D. L. Moody had built was destroyed, including his church and home. Before the fire was contained, it destroyed eighteen hundred buildings. Ninety thousand were left homeless and three hundred died.

But God turned that tragedy into an opportunity. Moody immediately began raising money to rebuild. In less than three months, the Northside Tabernacle was constructed to accommodate the work temporarily. It became a hub for the ministry of the gospel to the community. From that great crisis was birthed a single-focused desire for evangelism, greater power in his preaching, and a greater harvest of souls.[3]

What setback in your life could become a ministry? What trial could open up a new dimension of truth? What failure could result in your seeking God and walking by faith like never before?

Above all, no matter what crisis comes your way, seek Christ in the midst of the fire.

Fire Drill!

1. How do you typically react when a crisis arises? Does it usually help the situation?

2. What are some tools you can use in dealing with crises in the future?

3. How can a crisis, a trial, benefit us?

4. Make a list of past conflicts. Then list what you have learned from each one of them.

5. Take some time now to thank God for each of the conflicts you've faced and what you've learned from each of them.

CHAPTER 10

A Fireproof Eternity

Each one's work will become obvious, for the day
will disclose it, because it will be revealed by fire; the
fire will test the quality of each one's work.
—1 CORINTHIANS 3:13

These pages contain a great deal about fireproofing your life. As you've learned, having a fireproof life does not mean we will avoid the fire. It means we've made preparations for the fiery trials that will inevitably come.

Computer firewalls accomplish this very purpose. Because we know that viruses and inappropriate material can come into our homes through the Internet, we set up firewalls and filters to block a host of destructive content.

The Internet connection travels into your computer through multiple ports, and a firewall allows you to turn ports on and off to control the traffic into your home. Without a firewall, you expose yourself and others to the flames.

Ultimately, for the believer and nonbeliever, there will be a fire. The unbeliever will be cast into the everlasting flames. The believer's fire is of a different nature: Our works will be tried "as by fire," according to Paul's instructions to the Corinthians.

Paul wrote, "For we must all appear before the tribunal of Christ, so that each may be repaid for what he has done in the body, whether good or worthless" (2 Corinthians 5:10). This verse compares the judgment of believers to the Greek Olympic games, where the ruler, governor, or judge sat on a "bema"—a raised platform—to address the crowd, grant awards, or render a verdict. It was the place where a case was heard and a ruling rendered by one in authority. No bribes or grading on a curve. We will stand alone before the Judge of glory to hear His verdict on our work as believers.

Preparing for Eternity

In *Fireproof*, one of the firefighters, Wayne, overhears the conversation between Michael and Eric (page 137), and he wants to know more.

INT. FIRE HALL
WAYNE and CALEB gather their things after the accident, walk between the two fire trucks.

WAYNE

Hey, Cap'n. Hold up for a second.
CALEB stops, turns to WAYNE.

WAYNE

You know where you're going?

CALEB

(quizzical look) I'm going to my office.

WAYNE

Nah. (pauses, shakes head) You believe
in heaven and hell?

CALEB

(sighs, shrugs) I don't know.

WAYNE

When I die, I'm going in the ground.
And that's where I'm staying.

CALEB

(smiles) You know, you and Michael both
seem so sure, but one of you is wrong.

WAYNE

(laughs) It ain't me.

CALEB

(smiles) How do you know? (pauses) Hey, listen,
you might not agree with Michael.
But you and I both know: he's the real deal.

WAYNE crosses arms leans back against fire
truck. CALEB walks toward office.

Whether we realize it or not, we are one breath, one heartbeat away from our rewards, whether joy or embarrassment. There are no second runs; this isn't a dress rehearsal. We live, we die, then we live again for eternity.

Are you living now what you want to be then? Or are you living as if you've got all the time in the world to get your act together?

We must realize now that this life is preparation for eternity. The judgment seat of Christ will be a day of accounting when all Christians must appear. Not a few. Not just the preachers. All who have received salvation from Christ. And we must ask ourselves, *What am I doing to prepare for judgment? Am I being a good steward with what I have, working in God's will?*

On that day, our works will be judged. Our true motives will be revealed and our true character examined. Paul said each man's work will be "revealed by fire" (1 Corinthians 3:13). Anything selfish or petty will burn up.

How can we pass the ultimate fire test? What do we need to learn in this life that will prepare us for this test in the next? Have you made the necessary preparations to stand before Christ in judgment?

The emphasis is on motives, not achievements. Titles and degrees will burn up. Only that which brings honor and glory to Jesus Christ will survive.

Our works don't get us to heaven, but they follow us there.

Although we are not saved by works, we *are* rewarded for

them. That's good news! We were created in Christ Jesus to do good works. Our works don't get us to heaven, but they follow us there.

Our Desperate Need

Although I want to do all I can to live a fireproof life, I also want to do all I can to keep a different kind of fire burning—the fire in my heart. I want to be like the two on the road to Emmaus: "Weren't our hearts ablaze within us . . . ?" (Luke 24:32). I want to have a burning heart for God. I want to finish well.

The issues addressed in this book are real. They are common areas where the battle rages—traps that have captured and wounded many believers along the journey. The lives of Noah, Moses, the prophets, and the apostles show us that storms will come for the godly. A fireproof life means that we can survive the test and live as overcomers even in the toughest times.

We'll never live a fireproof life, however, if we are consumed with pleasing this present age. There has never been a culture since the dawn of the church in which a Christian could feel at home. But don't make the mistake of hoping for heaven while acting like the world.

We are to be in the world but not of it. We are saved out of the world to take the gospel back into the world and bring others out of the world—and the cycle continues. We are pilgrims. Strangers. Exiles. Aliens. We're on a journey.

And we should pray for God's keeping power until we reach our destination.

Today, more than ever, we need that power. We often shrivel at the first sign of testing and trials. We shrink back when the world confronts us. The highway is littered with fallen followers.

Think about it. It's not hard to think of the name of some athlete, politician, or preacher who was once used by God but blew it somewhere along the road. They had so much in their favor, but they fell morally or ethically. Now when you hear their names, all you think about is their failure. The good has been snuffed out by their poor decisions.

Some consider afflictions to be a training class in the school of faith. Others, because they have not guarded their hearts and minds in Christ Jesus, see their troubles as reminders of failure. But afflictions, tests, and trials are often God's blessings in disguise.

As gold is tried and refined by fire, so the fires of adversity reveal the sincerity of our faith. Many of us can testify that the fire burned away impurities, enabling us to grow purer in our spiritual lives. As the hammer forges steel, so the tests of life forge our faith. There can be no triumphs without a trial.

There can be no triumphs without a trial.

We have a long way to go on our journey. We don't need any more casualties. We need young men and women who can stand in the storms of life—fireproof believers who will arrive with their testimony intact.

Will you be one of them?

Fire Drill!

1. What is one trial you've experienced that has made you a better person today?

2. Can you imagine what our final judgment will be like? What are some things that you think God will reward you for?

3. What are some ways that you can keep the fire in your heart burning for Christ?

4. What have you done to fireproof your life for eternity? Do you know that you'll be spending it in heaven? If not, make it a point to talk to a pastor or Christian mentor about it. Do it *today*.

5. What can you do every day to keep your mind focused on an eternal perspective?

A Fireproof Legacy

As a teenager, I didn't really put a lot of thought into the legacy I would leave. In fact, I didn't put a lot of thought into leaving this earth at all. But now, as a father of grown daughters, leaving a lasting legacy has gained a whole new level of importance.

So take it from this old guy, who was *once* a teenager, the legacy that you are building—right this very moment—*matters*. It will matter for you. It will matter for your children. It will matter for your grandchildren. And their children.

What does that legacy look like right now? With the choices you made today? Yesterday? Last week?

Do you want my opinion? Unless you just randomly flipped to this page, I'd say you're off to a pretty good start.

You've just chosen to spend your time reading, to the very end, a book about building a life that lasts, a life that will long outlast the earthly bounds of death.

But I challenge you, I *beg* you: don't stop there.

Dig deeper. Keep going. Keep studying. Keep spending time with God and in His Word. Use these tools, these lessons, this newfound fireproofing of your life to affect the world around you.

Back at the beginning, I talked about the amazing sequoias and how they represented a fireproof life. My friend Ken's photography inspired a whole new understanding of being fireproof. I was especially struck by a fascinating fact he learned while photographing the trees.

While Ken and the forester were talking, a massive sequoia fell, landing with a thundering force that shook the ground. The forester explained that the giant tree did not fall because of the hundreds of past fires that had attacked it over the course of its long life. The tree fell because it had simply reached the full extent of its life.

But even in death, the tree has a life-giving function: to expose fertile soil and to provide nutrients to other plants and animals. The other plants and animals affected by this tree would thrive as a result of the tree's long-standing faithfulness to its call.

In the same way, those who have lived their lives to the glory of God will continue to bear fruit, even in death. Their lives make an impact that still resonates in the forest of the faithful.

Think of those who have gone before you, whose lives still continue to challenge you to be holy and know Christ more fully. You can become one of them—starting now.

Each of us has been entrusted with a great spiritual heritage. The giants of the past may have fallen. But they have left their books, messages, and wisdom as an investment in the soil of our hearts.

What will you leave behind?

Today is our day. This is our time. Will we grow into giants of faith, standing tall through the fires, for all to look up to?

Will we stand tall as an example of a fireproof life?

Start leaving your legacy *now*. Live with eternity in mind. Through the fun times and the fires, let every moment of your life be an example of fireproof faith.

Notes

Chapter 1: Standing in the Fire

1. Ken Jenkins is the source of the sequoia material in this book. For more information about Ken's ministry through photography and speaking, visit kenjenkins.com.

Chapter 2: Fireproof Your Life—Right Now!

1. "A Man You Would Write About," written by Billy Simon, © 1990 Locally Owned Music (BMI) River Oaks Music Company (BMI) (adm. at CapitolCMGPublishing.com) All rights reserved. Used by permission.

Chapter 3: A Fireproof Faith

1. Ron Dunn, *The Faith Crisis* (Nashville: B&H Books, 2013), 5.

2. Ibid., 18.

3. All quotes from *The Complete Gathered Gold* (Darlington, UK: Evangelical Press, 2006).

4. Warren Wiersbe, *Bible Exposition Commentary* (Wheaton, IL: Victor Books, 1989), digital edition (CD).

5. *The Complete Gathered Gold* (Darlingtonm UK: Evangelical Press, 2006).

6. Ibid.

7. Jim Cymbala, *Fresh Faith: What Happens When Real Faith Ignites God's People* (Grand Rapids, MI: Zondervan, 1999).

Chapter 4: Fireproof Your Heart and Mind

1. Vance Havner, *Reflections on the Gospels*, ed. Michael Catt (Xulon Press, 2003).

2. Robert D. Spender, article in *Evangelical Dictionary of Biblical Theology* (Grand Rapids, MI: Baker Books, 1996).

3. J. B. Lightfoot, *St. Paul's Epistles to the Colossians and to Philemon* (Grand Rapids, MI: Zondervan, 1959 [reprint of 1879 ed.]), 209.

4. Wiersbe, *Bible Exposition Commentary*.

5. A. T. Robertson, *Paul and the Intellectuals* (Nashville: Broadman, 1959), 98.

6. These points are borrowed from Bill Elliff's publication by Life Action Ministries, "Personal Revivial Checklist." For more information, visit lifeaction.org.

Chapter 5: Fireproof Convictions

1. DJ Readers Report, *Discipleship Journal*, Issue 72 (Nov/ Dec 1992).

2. Chuck Swindoll, *The Finishing Touch* (Dallas, TX: Word, 1994), 580–81.

Chapter 6: Fireproof Decision-Making

1. From an article by Good News Publishers, date unknown.

2. Gary Inrig, *Hearts of Iron, Feet of Clay* (Chicago: Moody Press, 1979), 109–10.

3. Brother Lawrence, *The Practice of the Presence of God,* first letter.

Chapter 8: Fireproof Money

1. Bill Bright, *As You Sow* (San Bernadino, CA: Here's Life Publishers, 1989), 62.

2. Wiersbe, *Bible Exposition Commentary.*

Chapter 9: Fireproof—No Matter What

1. Emmett C. Murphy, *The Genius of Sitting Bull: Thirteen Heroic Strategies for Today's Business Leaders* (Englewood Cliffs, NJ: Prentice Hall, 1992).

2. John Mason, *Why Ask Why? If You Know the Right Questions You Can Find the Right Answers* (Gainesville, FL: Bridge-Logos, 2000).

3. William R. Moody, *The Life of D. L. Moody* (New York: Macmillan, 1930), 131.

Acknowledgments

There is no such thing as a self-made man. Anyone who finds some measure of success has done it because of a partnership with others. It is the "others" who have invested in us who make us who we are. Without them, we would be limited in our focus, understanding, and impact.

Ken Jenkins provided the inspiration for this book. He is a *National Geographic* award-winning photographer and one of the most godly men I have ever known. His photography is second to none. His awareness of God in creation (Romans 1:20) is inspiring. I'm eternally grateful for Ken's willingness to share the story of the sequoias in this book. You can learn more about Ken's work at kenjenkins.com.

Without the folks at CLC who first published *Fireproof Your Life* and who first believed in me as an author, I would still be a frustrated writer. And without the vision of Dan

Lynch and B&H Kids, my *Fireproof* principles would have never made it into the hands of teens.

The members of Sherwood Baptist Church, where I've had the privilege of pastoring for nearly twenty-five years, have prayed for me, encouraged me, and at times, tolerated me. I know without a doubt that their prayers have shielded me in and from many fires.

Debbie Toole has been my administrative assistant for over twenty years. She makes sure I'm where I'm supposed to be when I'm supposed to be there. She is a Godsend to me and my ministry. Stephanie Bennett, my research assistant, helped me pull this material together and made the initial edits and corrections. Stephanie is diligent in all she does and makes me look like I actually passed my grammar classes.

It has been a joy to work with Amy Parker once again. I am grateful for the talents God has given her in helping me communicate this message to a younger audience. Amy's tireless work has left a lasting legacy for the next generation.

My wife, Terri, reminded me of numerous stories and situations that I had forgotten in the first draft. Without her input, this book would be lacking. Our older daughter, Erin, is living for Christ as an actress and entertainer. She has seen up close and personal the effects of work associates who play with fire. Our younger daughter, Hayley, was our church photographer on the set of *Fireproof*. Her pictures have been used in numerous publications, and you can see them at fireproofthemovie.com. She's using her photographer's eye to capture images to be used for the glory of God.

Two preachers have invested much in me in recent years. God allowed me to get to know Warren Wiersbe in the mid-1990s, and he has been a constant source of encouragement. His wisdom and insights are invaluable. I never talk to him when I don't have a pen in hand. His nuggets of truth off the top of his head reveal a deep mine full of riches learned at the feet of Jesus. I am listening and learning from one of God's giants.

I have known Tom Elliff for a long time. In recent years, he has become a key adviser, friend, and confidant. I've watched him walk through the fires of ministry from a distance and up close. He is a man you would want to walk with through a fire. Tom models for me the Spirit-filled life that can survive life's fires.

I am blessed to have prayer warriors in the church and around the country. These individuals have covered me in ways only eternity will reveal. Paul said it best in his letter to the Philippians: "What does it matter? Just that in every way, whether out of false motives or true, Christ is proclaimed. And in this I rejoice. Yes, and I will rejoice because I know this will lead to my deliverance through your prayers and help from the Spirit of Jesus Christ" (1:18–19). We need both. I need both. To live a fireproof life, I am desperate for the prayers of the saints and the provision of the Spirit. I know in glory I will praise God for my deliverance from fires the Enemy set for me because of the prayer that bombarded heaven on my behalf and because of the provisions of the Spirit of Christ.

There are many casualties in the family of God. Some warm themselves at the Enemy's fire, while others play with fire. Many foolishly think they are fireproof in their own strength. This book is written with the prayer that we will all finish well. Although the fires will come, we can make preparations for them. We don't have to be casualties or statistics. We can do more than survive. My prayer for you is that God would use these pages, along with the prayers of the saints and the provision of the Spirit, to see you safely home.

Blessings,
Michael Catt
MichaelCatt.com

Again, I am honored to read, adapt, and learn firsthand these lessons from Michael Catt. It has been such a privilege to help get this message out to the teens just beginning to develop their fireproof lives. And it has helped me in galvanizing my own.

Thank you to Bill Reeves, Brian Mitchell, and Working Title Agency for always finding the right fit for my writing. And to Dan Lynch, whose grace and patience and ability to encourage are infinite.

Immeasurable appreciation goes to my husband, Daniel, and my two sweet boys, Michael and Ethan—who somehow tolerate the roller coaster of the writing life. But I pray that on this last ride, you have learned alongside me about how to fireproof your life. At the very least, I hope that you see it lived out by example in my own.

To my Father in heaven, who supplies all of my words and guides me through His, all of this is Yours and for You.

And an enormous thank-you and admiration goes to the teens who have the drive and courage to read this book. If you are feeling the fire, press on. Push through. You will find a more faith-filled life waiting on the other side.

Love,
Amy Parker
Amyparkerbooks.com

About the Authors

Michael Catt has served as Senior Pastor of Sherwood Baptist Church in Albany, Georgia, since 1989 and is Executive Producer of the popular films *Flywheel, Facing the Giants, Fireproof,* and *Courageous* that originated from the congregation. He also authored *Fireproof Your Life, Courageous Living,* and *Courageous Teens* and founded the ReFRESH® revival conference. Michael and his wife, Terri, have two children.

Amy Parker has written more than twenty books for children, teens, and adults, including the best-selling *A Night Night Prayer, Thank You, God, for Mommy,* and *Thank You, God, for Daddy.* She has also collaborated with authors ranging from *New York Times* best sellers to her very own son. Two of these collaborations—*Firebird* and *Courageous Teens*—are recipients of Christian Retailing's Best Awards. But Amy's greatest reward is being a wife to Daniel and a mom to their amazing sons, Michael and Ethan.

YOU NEED COURAGE

TO LIVE FOR GOD.

TO FAITHFULLY LEAD YOUR GENERATION.

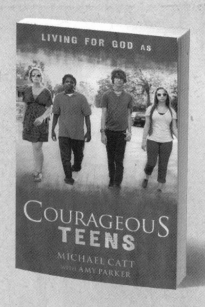

Courageous Teens is a student-focused presentation of *Courageous Living* by Michael Catt, senior pastor of Sherwood Baptist Church and executive producer of the hit film COURAGEOUS.

Catt brings fresh insight to "stories of people in the Bible who displayed great courage when it would have been easier to play it safe . . . (who) challenge me to keep moving forward. They demand that I examine my priorities and deal with anything that brings fear to my heart."

Teen readers will be inspired to resolve to live for God as they learn more about Abraham, Moses, Nehemiah, Ruth, Daniel, and many more.

Best-selling youth market author Amy Parker arranges the heart-stirring material into four categories: Courageous Faith, Courageous Leadership, Courageous Priorities, and Courageous Influence. Discussion questions are also included at the end of each chapter.

Every WORD Matters™
BHPublishingGroup.com